Unclaimed Soul

A Memoir

Patti Callahan

www.auctuspublishers.com

AucTus Publishers

For Quinn and Drake – the loves of my life

Table of Contents

Prologue

I do not matter.

For the first 25 years of my life, this was all I knew. By the time I was seven, this truth was a bad tattoo inked indelibly on my soul. It was evident daily in a million ways both large and small. I wholeheartedly believed I was difficult to love. I had to be, because the ones who were supposed to love me the most made it clear that I was, at best, tolerated. It is a message that has taken a lifetime to erase.

My childhood is a blur of unhappiness and pain. I alternated between trying to be invisible and screaming from the rooftops for attention. Why didn't I matter? Why did no one show me love or affection? Why was everything so hard? Obedience was the expectation. Do as you are told. Don't make waves. Don't ask for anything other than what you are given. We did not do joy or happiness in our home; we did control. Always control.

I spent more than a decade of young adulthood trying to reclaim my worth in the unhealthiest of ways. I was an addict. Not to drugs or alcohol, but to needing to be wanted, to be chosen. I chased friends, boyfriends, and eventually husbands, believing I would finally feel okay if someone picked me. I begged people not to leave so I could avoid feeling abandoned and unimportant. It didn't matter if having them in my life was good for me. All I knew was that I could not handle yet another reminder that I was not enough and that no one would ever choose me. I happily accepted scraps of love and affection from nearly anyone who offered just so I could feel chosen and special. I made so many excuses for lies and disrespectful treatment. I felt myself believing that pain and uncertainty was always how love would be for someone like me. I rationalized behavior that should have sent me running for the door. And I did it all because I knew I didn't have the right to ask for anything more.

I spent years actively trying to change who I was to be accepted. It seemed a perfectly logical thing to do since being myself was getting me nowhere, and the problem could not possibly be anything else. I minimized the things that made me happy out of fear they were not exciting enough. I genuinely believed that my love of books, dislike of sports, and need for solitude meant I was boring. I knew in my heart that no one would want a life with someone so dull. Time and again, I chose relationships of all kinds with people who would validate that belief. It was a never-ending cycle of pain that reinforced a core truth: I was worthless.

It has taken years of hard work to develop the tools and find the courage to challenge beliefs borne from a childhood of destructive messages. It has taken even longer to get to a place where I can forgive myself for the anger and bitterness that I held onto like a life raft in a raging sea. Because if I forgive myself, then what? How do I survive if I let go of all the pain? Who am I, if not the invisible, unmemorable, unimportant person I had always been? Pain was the only steady, consistent thing I knew. It defined me as much or more than anything else in my life. I referenced it at the start of every new relationship, trying – generally in vain – to be heard, seen, understood.

Navigating conflict was always a challenge. Trying to balance speaking up with a paralyzing fear of being abandoned for doing so was a tightrope I was always about to fall from. As a child and then a teen, I was not afraid of it. I argued, I pushed back, I stood up for myself. It did not bring good results. Instead, standing up for myself brought only a steady stream of punishments and a family reputation as the bad kid. Ultimately, I came to associate using my voice with being bad when I so very desperately wanted to be liked. Is it any wonder that I grew to be anxious, insecure, and afraid of showing my emotions? As an adult, I learned to freeze. To fear conflict. To fear that if I were "difficult" then I wouldn't be worth the effort. I knew wholeheartedly if I just stayed quiet and amenable, someone would finally stay.

Failed marriages were inevitable. Why would someone want me? And for a lifetime? It made no sense, and soon my self-loathing became a self-fulfilling prophecy. Partners rightfully struggle to understand when an epic meltdown over a miscommunication is really pain from a lifetime of feeling invisible and being unable to find the words, or the courage, to say so.

Eventually, after years of searching for hope and working at healing, I came to realize that the only way out was to let go. I had stayed so long in the dark, hanging on to my pain, because it was all I knew. I was terrified by the unknown. The constant hurt of my daily life had become comforting in its predictability. It was steady and solid.

I knew what to expect, and that felt safe. Pain was my home.

Finally, I started asking what would happen if I gave up every truth I knew. If I decided that the toxic messages playing on a nonstop loop were wrong. What would happen if I dared to challenge them and change my life in the process? If I started listening to the other messages, the hopeful and forgiving ones delivered by the familiar, trusted voices, or by the strangers who briefly crossed my path, or even from my own intuition, would I finally find peace?

This is the story of that journey.

Part I: The Darkness

Hidden truths are unspoken lies
— Tang

Psychic

My first encounter with a psychic was in 1991. Psychic is probably an inaccurate title since she didn't consider herself one. She didn't advertise or charge. She didn't even like people to know about that side of her, but that didn't change the fact that she knew things. I was working as a hairstylist, she was a regular client of mine, and over time our conversations shifted from normal chit chat about her life to what was going on in mine.

I was still in emotional recovery both from being abused in high school and a disaster of a childhood. I didn't yet have the vocabulary or understanding to know that the coworker who forced himself on me in his waterbed while I was drunk two years earlier had, in fact, committed a crime. All I knew was that I was desperate to not feel different anymore. I wanted to be normal. Eventually, while waiting for her hair color to process, we talked about my hurdles getting started in adulthood.

I remember this client as the first person to tell me that my voice and my experiences mattered. She told me that I have power in and over my life, and to trust people's actions over their words every time. Those bits of wisdom alone are enough for me to value her forever, regardless of how one feels about the term "psychic", or what she told me next.

She told me that she saw three great loves in my life. The first, she said, will feel especially important, but it's young love and will fade. The second, she warned, will be the hardest. He will seem to be everything I want, and I will feel certain that he is the one. But, she said, without question, he's not. Everything about him and the relationship will be a lie. She urged me to have the courage to wait because my great love would be number three. She described him as a good, kind man with ties to South Carolina who would be everything. That man, she said, he's your love. Wait for him.

I didn't put a lot of stock into the three loves stuff. I just liked how calm and matter of fact she was about life. It was so different from the dramatic martyrdom of my mom, and far less pragmatic and analytical than my therapist.

The last time I saw this client, she told me again of the importance of believing in myself and my value. She reminded me of great love number three and begged me to not trust the second because it would only lead to pain. That day I asked her why she didn't make a living doing readings. She told me she would have a hard time standing before God one day saying she took money for a gift He gave her.

Over the years, life moved on and she largely faded from my mind. I shared her predictions with friends now and then but didn't put a lot of energy into it otherwise. But when my marriage to husband number two was starting to implode, one of those friends remembered her and asked if I thought he was love number two.

I had no doubt.

Daddy Issues

I have a theory that all women have daddy issues, and that not all are bad. The best come from dads who love and raise their girls with the confidence to know who they are and to wait for someone to treat them right. The only issue with that is finding a partner who can measure up. For these daughters, it's more blessing than baggage, but you get my point: none of us escapes the legacies of our fathers, good or bad.

My parents divorced before I started kindergarten, so my younger sister and I were raised primarily by my mom during our early childhood years. I have very few memories of Mom and Dad together. None of them are good.

The first memory of my life is Mom sitting on the side of the bed in her housecoat crying, trying to keep calm while Dad threatened and accused her of horrible things. I remember him hitting her. I remember him ordering her to take her clothes off. I remember her scared face when she told me to go back to bed after seeing me in the door-way. He saw me, too, and angrily ordered me to get out. I don't remember exactly what happened after, but I do have very clear memories of him in the kitchen shoving her and ripping the olive-green rotary dial phone off the wall in a rage when she tried to call for help.

I don't remember if the police came that day. I know they did on many other occasions. Sometimes, my sister and I were sent next door to stay with the neighbors while the police took Dad outside to talk. As if talking to wife-beaters ever made them stop.

As far as I know, Dad was never arrested for beating Mom. It was the seventies and domestic violence was still very much considered a "family matter". The police would come, everyone would be talked to, and they would leave us to go about our lives. I don't know if it was after that beating or after another, but eventually Mom packed up and left with me and my sister, Erica.

I will always be grateful to her for finding the courage to leave. So much of my survival spirit comes from my mom as she was in those years. At first, every day was hard. We were welfare-and-food-stamp poor, but we were safe, and Mom was transformed. Eventually, she was happy again. I loved those days. They were the best years of my childhood and form most of the few happy memories I have of growing up.

Years passed, and Mom and Dad both remarried. Mom married my kindergarten teacher, a man that I adored and the person who taught me to read. But their marriage was brief – barely long enough to have my brother Steven – and soon it was just us and Mom once again. Dad moved away during that time and chose to become a summer-break only parent. We rarely heard from him and saw him even less. I can't begin to count the number of times Mom said he was coming for a visit or to take us for the weekend. Erica and I would be so excited, packing bags and making plans, happy to be seeing Dad. As the day drew closer, and for reasons that were never quite clear, visits were inevitably canceled, sometimes mere hours before.

Over time, I came to expect nothing from him, while still being crushed that my own dad didn't want me. Once, in what I'm sure was an attempt at comfort, Mom told me if I had one parent who loved me, I had enough. I disagreed, but it wasn't a topic open for discussion.

When I was fourteen, during what ended up being one of our last visitation trips, I noticed Dad hardly looked at me. He and Erica seemed to have an easy, natural father-daughter rapport. But with me, it was awkward. Little to no eye contact. Minimal conversation. Nothing in common. I didn't know why we struggled to connect. All I knew was it felt like more proof that something was wrong with me. Years later, during the heavy rationalization phase of my healing, I decided he wouldn't look at me because I looked so much like my mom. I have no idea if there's truth to that, but it made me feel better.

The day I graduated from high school, anxiety and fear took over as I hoped against hope that he would show up to see me get my diploma. He'd been invited, of course, but was still prone to last minute cancellations. He walked in at the last possible moment, just as the band was playing the first notes of "Pomp and Circumstance." I ran to hug him, tears flooding my eyes, wanting nothing more than for Daddy to be proud. I was in heaven that day. My dad showed up for me, the little girl no one seemed to want. Dad even stayed for the reception at my parents' house. My graduation gift was a set of tires. My dad loved me so much that he wanted me safe on the road! Proof that I mattered! I only saw him a few more times after that. He remained a ghost who only existed in the periphery of his daughters' lives.

At nineteen, through tears during a deeply emotional phone call, I asked, "why did you leave us?"

His answer was simple and heartbreaking. "I know I was a piss poor father," he said. "It was just easier to let whoever your mother was married to raise you guys." That was it. Being Dad was too much work, so he punted.

When I was twenty-five and in the early months of pregnancy with my oldest, my now ex-husband and I stopped to see him while on a road trip. After a few moments of our usual super awkward conversation, I told him I was expecting.

He looked at me without emotion and said, "Is it too late to have an abortion?"

My husband didn't hear him. If he had, there would have been bloodshed. I stood there, numb, staring at him while I tried to figure out what to say. Was he joking? Was this just an awful attempt at humor? I'll never know. At that point in my life, I was fully conflict-averse and never asked. I remember making a confused, undefinable sound then changing the subject. We left moments later but the damage was done.

"How hard would it have been to say congratulations?" I asked my husband as we drove away. It's not like I was asking for permission, or a blessing, or even cash. He'd handed me forty dollars on my way out the door, though. To this day, I don't know if it was guilt or gas money.

Would he have said the same thing to my sister, who was also pregnant at the time? Would he utter those words to his stepdaughter, the one who called him Dad and was the recipient of all the love and attention I didn't get? No, I told myself, he would only say it to me because I don't matter, and they do.

He's seen my oldest son once, as an infant and only for a moment, and has never met my youngest. My kids refer to him by first name only, and with disdain, on the rare occasions he comes up. To them, their grandpa is my stepdad, the man who raised me. I am more than fine with that. They deserve better than a man who handed off his daughters to whoever their mom married.

A decade later, newly married to husband number two, I decided I needed to purge the last of my anger toward my father. I hadn't seen him in nearly twelve years by then, but I could feel the lingering effects of the wreckage still creating havoc in my life. It was time to let go.

Since we didn't speak, and as I was still in the earliest stages of relearning to use my voice, I wrote him a letter. I said everything I needed to say. I minced no words and pulled no punches. I ended it with "fuck you," mailed it, and then happily shut the door on that chapter. The release felt amazing. I was certain my daddy issues were fully healed and put to rest.

Nope. Turns out I still had some work to do. This time with my stepdad.

I met my stepdad when I was seven. He and Mom married when I was ten and then we all moved to the small town where he grew up. While he is my mom's third husband, he had never been married before and had no children. As I got older, I came to appreciate how much he took on – three kids and a twice-divorced wife – but in the early years, it was a struggle.

As with my dad, it was always tense and awkward between my stepdad and me. We butted heads a lot. I didn't like him, and he didn't really like me. I remember him telling me more than once I was part of the package he had to take on when he married my mom. I think he meant it better than I heard it, but it came out badly and I took it as more proof that I was unwanted and didn't matter. It was another reminder that I wasn't worth anything on my own and that I was only there because he had no choice in the matter. Of course, It didn't help that he was mean. It's hard to say that about him now because he's the sweetest grandfather in the world and genuinely loves me as his own. But I'm confident he'd agree the first twenty years of our relationship were not good.

Growing up, I was always guarded around him and certain I was about to get in trouble for some unknown something. I was usually right. The energy in our house would shift when we heard him come up the front steps. The tension was palpable as we all waited to see what mood – and what version of him – would greet us. He was never violent, but he was angry a lot and in a bad mood almost all the time. The man hated his job, and I'm guessing felt incredibly stressed as the sole provider for what had quickly become a family of seven after the births of my youngest siblings. That frustration naturally played out at home. It sucked.

I resented how he treated me and came to refer to him as "the man my mother married". I would neither say his name nor call him my stepdad. We remained in a mostly silent cold war that lasted into my early twenties, except for occasional battles that got ugly fast.

We had no meaningful parent-child connection, and I was fine with that. Having already lost a dad and my first stepdad, I was in no great rush to build a bond with yet another father figure. Lucky for me, he connected easily with Erica and mostly opted out of trying to be my dad. Once my youngest siblings were born, there was no need to try to treat me as one of his kids. I was his wife's daughter and nothing more. I was also perfectly content when we settled into mostly ignoring each other. It certainly beat getting in trouble all the damn time.

Our relationship breakthrough finally came when I was moving into a new house following my own divorce. He had slowly started warming to me once I became a parent, having fallen madly in love with his grandchildren. It felt like he decided maybe I wasn't as bad as he and Mom had made me out to be for so many years. It was a nice change. Plus, he adored my boys. They had him wrapped around their fingers. It was so sweet watching him with them and seeing him take such joy in being part of their lives. Stepdad as grandpa was nothing like stepdad as parent. He had retired from the job he hated and was genuinely enjoying his life. It seemed to make all the difference in his relationships.

That day, while Mom and I unpacked the house, he set about installing my washer and dryer. I went downstairs to check on progress and to thank him for his help.

With tears in his eyes, he said, "I am a man who owns my mistakes and I try to make things right whenever I can. I have a lot to make right with you, I'm sorry for how I treated you as a child. It was not okay." He hugged me, and said he loved me for the first time ever. I was in shock and could not say it back. But I did cry with him, and I did thank him.

Today our relationship is as good as it will ever be. We don't have a traditional father-daughter connection. I don't have that with anyone, and don't know if I am wired for it. But I did forgive him. I do love him. I am so grateful for the grandfather he has been to my sons. In the end, that's all the healing and peace that bond needed.

Mommy Issues

I've been semi-estranged from my mom my entire adult life and our only real connection is my kids. Beyond that, we don't have a relationship, which is equal parts sad and in the best interest of my mental health. The only way I can love her is from a distance.

Much like my stepdad, she's amazing as a grandparent. My kids adore her, which I love, and the feeling is more than mutual. She's earned lasting love, gratitude, and respect from me in that area. But to give that, I must compartmentalize. Separate the behavior of the grandmother she became from that of the mother she was. The remainder of this chapter is about my mom, not my kids' grandmother—two very different people sharing the same human form.

In any crisis requiring tangible action, Mom is wonderful. She has picked up grandkids on short notice and she has supported them wholeheartedly by attending all the sports and school events. She has even offered short term emergency loans in times of divorce, surgery, or other major life happenings. However, accepting her help binds her children to an implicit contract. She gets to share all details of our life with whomever she pleases, however she pleases. There's nothing in it for her unless she can advertise her role as Supermom.

What Mom will not do, what she cannot do, is provide emotional support. She is wholly incapable. Being open and vulnerable with her means knowingly contributing to stockpiles of emotional ammunition that will be weaponized for later use. Shots are generally fired during conversations intended to hold her accountable or reestablish a boundary. She will absolutely use those weapons to lash out at her own children if it serves her. I have known this about her my entire life, as have my siblings. As adults, we all limit what we tell her because we have all been burned. Simply put, Mom lives in a bubble that is all about her. In her bubble she can do what she wants, how she wants, and regularly rewrite history to suit the mood of the day. In her version of life, she is always a victim or a martyr. There is no in-between.

It was difficult growing up as the oldest and the lookalike daughter of a woman hardwired to make everything all about her. My wins, which were few, were nothing but a reflection of her love and devoted parenting. My losses, which were many, were ignored or rewritten so that her pain as the parent watching me suffer was greater. For years, it felt like her mission in life was to create in me a younger version of herself.

Mom was paranoid and obsessive about control, and I didn't know then that her behavior was unhealthy. I thought that was just how you showed love. I had no idea that betraying the trust of your children and sharing their secrets was the definition of untrustworthy. She was my mother. I believed it was her absolute right to do what she wanted with whatever she knew about me or my life. If there were consequences or fallout from what she shared about me, I believed it was my fault for choosing to share with her in the first place.

Mom grew less controlling and overzealous with each child. I'm not sure why. Maybe it was the natural mellowing that comes from having multiple children. Maybe it was sheer exhaustion from having five kids in twelve years. Or maybe it was because none of them looked as much like her as I did. Whatever the reason, by the time Natasha, my youngest sibling, was born, Mom had changed. She was disconnected from parenting for the most part, simply going through the motions. She still wanted credit for being all-things-maternal and was still unable to provide emotional support, but the paranoid need for total control seemed to have waned.

As a young adult, I was insanely jealous of my younger siblings for being raised by this different version of Mom. They never saw the nasty, manipulative, cruel side of her I did. They felt support and a bit of engagement instead of control and detachment. They didn't grow up uncertain if they were loved or resented. They didn't have seeds of doubt about their worth planted in them from the beginning. With me, she was always at extremes. I was the doppelgänger trotted out as a show pony, or I was the out-of-control bad kid held as an example for my siblings of what not to be.

I got good grades. I preferred to sit in a corner with a book and generally just be left alone. I didn't smoke, drink, do drugs, sneak out of the house, or do much of anything that most would consider rebellious. None of that mattered, though. I was always treated as the one who needed to be controlled. For some reason, I was never seen as the one who just needed love, acceptance, and stability.

My mom and I do look a lot alike, but I remember being completely embarrassed and wishing to be invisible when she erased my entire identity anytime someone commented on the physical resemblance. Without fail, she would light up and deliver the same nonsensical response, "She's my little carbon copy. Got her right off the Xerox." It was important that people knew I did not exist apart from her. Hobbies and most after school activities were preselected, with a preference for things that focused on church and sewing or crafts. I was encouraged to be an active participant, but there was always a limit. The underlying message: learn and have fun, but not too much.

In the early and mid-eighties, afternoon talk shows and the media were obsessed with child molestation and repressed memories. I was involved in a youth group that brought young teens from other local churches together for activities and bible study. I enjoyed it at first. It was fun to meet people outside of our small little church group, and I craved the opportunity to socialize with kids who didn't go to my school. A few months after I joined, I had an opportunity to go out of state for a heavily chaperoned youth group retreat weekend. Mom was completely on board. She thought it would be a great idea. That is, until the youth group advisors shared that they would be caravanning with all the kids. The very idea of it triggered her paranoia. She told me I was not allowed to ride in the car with the male advisor because he could be a child molester. It wasn't the first time she'd made such a proclamation without any supporting rationale. She tended to believe all men were predators and interrogated us regularly about the behavior of any adult male in our lives.

Keep in mind, she did not know my youth group advisor and had no reason to think the worst. That didn't stop her. It never did. She thrived on assuming everyone outside of our house was a danger, setting up a core belief that has been incredibly damaging to my ability to trust others and my own judgement.

My youth group advisor was a kind and generous young man who was never inappropriate with the group. Unfortunately, that did not matter. Mom was convinced of the righteousness of her position and stood firm in her paranoia. Even worse, I was young and stupid and did not understand the power of words. During the final meeting before the retreat, I looked him in the face and told him exactly what Mom said. I thought for sure he'd see the absurdity of it all and laugh with me at how crazy moms can be. He didn't. Instead, I watched as his expression morphed from surprise to shock to pain and hurt, finally landing at utter disgust. My words – or rather my mom's words, carelessly repeated – were cruel and hurtful to someone who had been nothing but genuinely good and kind to me. He never spoke to me again.

In the end, Mom made me ride with one of her friends who she claimed was coincidentally headed to Portland at the same time. I had wanted to spend the weekend trying to have fun with my friends and learn more about the word of God. I spent it instead isolated and ashamed, hoping my advisor would forget what I'd said so I could go back to feeling like part of the group again. It didn't happen, of course. It couldn't.

That was my last youth group event. The shame made me surrender one of the few escapes I had from my unhappy home life. It also marked the beginning of the isolation that would mark my teen and young adult years. I couldn't be shamed if I didn't do anything or talk to anyone.

Eventually, I came to see that my mother's need for total control, her paranoia, and even her narcissism, weren't about me. It was the only way she knew to mask her own fears and her own pain. The damage to me was collateral and unintended, but no less severe.

Abuse, Violence, & Assault

I was in high school the first time I was abused. Riley was a classmate I became friends with for no reason other than she was hanging out with another friend, Darlene. We had nothing in common outside of our shared friend. I didn't care. All I cared about was not losing one of the few friends I had, so I dove in and hung on for years.

The dynamics between three of us were unbalanced from the start. It was clear I was the other friend. The outlier. The secondary one whose friendship with either was nowhere near as valuable as their friendship with each other. I didn't care. I needed friends, and friends who treated me as less than were better than no friends at all.

Ever the outsider, I happily accepted the condescension disguised as kindness. I didn't question the snarky comments and cutting observations coming from the mouths of these friends, who all the while claimed they cared and were just telling me the truth. It didn't matter that their truth made me feel horrible about myself. I believed they were right.

I believed they knew things about life and the world that I didn't. I believed they saw things in me that I was too stupid to see. I blindly accepted every single rationalization given when I spoke up about how their poor treatment made me feel. They were my friends. They cared about me. If they believed I deserved to be used, looked down on, ignored, and generally treated like shit, then I did.

I was unquestioning in my belief that I was worth nothing more than the treatment I received. I didn't care. I was used to being ignored or pitied. I was used to being looked down on. It was normal. My whole life had been defined by the narrative of me being the bad kid unworthy of anything other than the shit I was given. Who was I to push back? Why would I think this should be any different?

The shift from unhealthy friendship dynamic to abuse was incremental. A little bit of gaslighting here, a little isolation there. Within a few months, I was shut down from my life and cut off from everyone but them. I had grown tired of defending my friendships to classmates who thought they were weird and couldn't understand why we hung out. I got tired of defending them to my parents who didn't like anyone. In the span of a semester, I stopped talking to nearly everyone and shifted to autopilot. I went to school. I did my homework. I swallowed my feelings. I endured.

By the time the abuse turned violent, I was so detached from myself it didn't feel real. More importantly, it didn't feel like something I had the right to be upset about. I had chosen this friendship. Therefore, I had chosen this treatment.

I couldn't talk to anyone about it because there was no one to talk to. Home was miserable. Mom was wrapped up in herself and my stepdad was no fan of mine. I was isolated at school, having pulled away from other friends and activities. I'd stopped being involved at church after the youth retreat incident a year earlier. Telling someone wasn't an option anyway because I lived in a small conservative town and the chances of it not becoming hot gossip were zero. I wasn't worth the trouble exposing it would have stirred up. Armed with that truth, my survival plan became withdraw even more, endure what I must, and focus on how many months were left until I graduated and could start a new life.

If only it were that easy.

The mental intimidation turned into physical violence my senior year. The first time it happened, I was in the backseat of Riley's car, headed home from a spring night froyo run with Riley and Darlene. Whitesnake was playing on the radio. They were talking while I stared out the window, not really paying attention. At some point, the energy in the car shifted. Suddenly, I was in trouble for some unforgivable thing I had said or done at school. I don't remember exactly what, only that it seemed to involve me talking to a boy. Riley went on and on about how cruel I was. I was so confused. I remember wracking my brain trying to figure out what was so bad about talking to a boy in history class. We hadn't gone on a date. We hadn't flirted. We'd literally just talked like we had almost daily since fifth grade. What was wrong with that?

I knew without question Riley was right and what I had done was awful. What I didn't know was why. If I didn't know why, how could I make sure I didn't accidentally do it again? Maybe I needed to stop talking to boys altogether. Darlene, who was supposed to be my best friend, was riding shotgun and stayed completely silent as the verbal assault continued. I felt a knot in my stomach when the car stopped at a quiet spot at the top of a hill. I didn't know what was going on, but it was clear something bad was about to happen.

I was frozen. I couldn't move. Riley turned to face the backseat, pointed a cocked revolver to my forehead and said, "I bet this'll hurt less than what you did to me" then pulled the trigger.

The gun wasn't loaded.

Then, just as quickly as it started, it was over. The gun lowered and I sank back into the seat, shaking. Darlene stared out the window as Riley started the car and took me home. None of us said a word and we never talked about it again.

I normalized that and a handful of other violent incidents over the next few months. I even convinced myself the violence wasn't that bad. I told myself I'd done something to deserve it while doing everything I could to bury my emotions.

The violence escalated in the months after graduation, both in frequency and severity. I think it's because we were no longer tied to each other the way classmates are, and that triggered something in my abuser. Graduation meant moving on, going separate ways. It meant I had an opportunity to escape not only my miserable home life but the toxic mess this 'friendship' had become.

I was starting to feel something resembling happiness and hope by September. But as was the norm back then, it was pulled away before I got too close. I'd gone to a party and slept with a classmate. We were in one of the bedrooms when Riley burst through the door in a rage. My memory has been kind enough to block out the immediate aftermath, but I will never forget the look on the face of the poor boy I was with. And I will never forget the feelings of shame, embarrassment, humiliation, and guilt that had shadowed me like a raincloud for the better part of three years.

A few days after the party, Riley called and wanted to hang out to watch the Olympics. Diving was on that night. It was 1988 and Greg Louganis was the star of the show. Despite what had happened, it never occurred to me to say no. I was excited because it meant I'd get a chance to continue to apologize for the unforgivable sin of being a teenager who had sex. Riley was strangely calm and controlled when I arrived, which was terrifying. I knew how to deal with rages and outbursts. I did not know how to handle the eerie quiet facing me now. I was interrogated and made to feel so much shame. Riley viewed my actions as a nearly unforgivable betrayal. The only thing that would make it better was punishment and humiliation.

When Greg Louganis was hitting his head on the springboard in Seoul, I was hogtied on the floor in front of the TV. Riley had grabbed a terry-cloth bathrobe tie and wrapped one end around my neck. The other was tied around my ankle. I was crying and apologizing nonstop, begging to be let go. Every time I cried, she pulled my ankle, straightening my leg and causing the loop around my neck to tighten. When I wasn't being choked, I was hyperventilating. I swallowed my tears and did my best to quiet my breathing. I just wanted it to stop. I didn't want to die on a stranger's floor.

I lost all sense of time and still have no idea how long it lasted. Eventually, with no explanation, the torture stopped. Riley untied me and told me to get out. I ran for my car and nearly wrecked it driving the gravel roads to get home, destroying a tire on the way. I had been strangled for having sex, and still told myself I got what I deserved. I was shaking when I pulled into the driveway and sat in my car a few minutes before going inside.

As soon as I walked in, I was greeted by angry parents. Someone had seen me speeding and driving erratically then called them. They looked at my destroyed tire then lectured me for being irresponsible and said that I could not be trusted. While they talked, I kept pulling up the neck of my shirt to cover the redness and turning away from them so they wouldn't see. If they noticed the marks, or the bruises that appeared later, neither of them ever said a word.

It was two days after my eighteenth birthday.

I moved into my first apartment about a month later, hoping that geography would help bring it all to an end. It didn't, but I was beginning to compartmentalize more aggressively. Since I was too terrified to officially end the friendship, I did the next best thing and tried to manage how much time I had to spend in it. I gradually winnowed it down to just a few hours a week, at most. I felt like I owed it to Darlene to not sever the ties completely. I also still didn't have any other friends. But I was pulling away from the toxicity and doing what I could to break free, which helped me feel less imprisoned.

That winter, when my brake line was slashed, something I didn't discover until I was driving home on icy roads, I told myself it was an accident. I knew there was no way Riley was really trying to kill me.

It wasn't until I was on the kitchen floor with a knife to my throat, Riley's full body weight holding me down, that I believed I might be murdered. I'd had the brake line fixed a few days prior, but someone pulled the spark plug wires out of my distributor so I couldn't go to work. I'd called my parents because I couldn't afford to have someone fix my car and had no idea how to put the wires back myself. My stepdad came over to help and was just getting ready to leave when Riley showed up. Everyone played nice until my stepdad left. Within minutes, Riley was screaming, accusing me of blaming her for the issues with my car. I denied it. Over and over again I denied it. It didn't matter.

I don't remember exactly how I ended up on the floor. I remember the knife being on the counter because I'd used it to slice an apple and hadn't washed it. I remember Riley grabbing it and saying, "How fucking dare you try to make me look like the asshole." By that point, though, all my fight was gone. I was done trying to get away from it. I didn't want to deal with the shame and gossip anymore. I just wanted it all to be over. Maybe this was how it was supposed to end. After nearly three years of isolation and abuse, I was done. I stopped fighting back, closed my eyes, and turned my head to the side to give easier access to my throat.

For whatever reason, total surrender stopped the attack. Riley left and we never saw each other alone again. I was free.

Therapy

My mom put me in therapy at eighteen, after I finally told her what happened in high school. She listened without interruption until I got to the part of the story that really mattered to her, which was whether the abuse had been sexual. The violence and emotional destruction were awful, but not as important to her as whether I'd been touched.

Her only request for therapy was that I go three times. If I didn't see value after the third visit, she promised I could quit and swore she'd never bring it up again. If I wanted to continue, she would pay for every session with no time limit and no questions asked. To this day, I am grateful. The gift of therapy helped set the first blocks in the unbreakable foundation of my healing.

Even though I'd agreed to go, I didn't know how to do therapy. I'm naturally very private and I was terrified of finding the courage to be open and then feeling judged. I was also certain no one would understand. I was deep in the shame and secrecy phase of my trauma, with no understanding of how deep it ran. At the same time, I told myself daily that I was fine and really didn't need to talk to anyone. I believed therapy was for people who couldn't cope. Since I got out of bed every day and participated in my life, I was clearly handling it all perfectly well.

I went with the sole intent of keeping my word to my mom. She did the legwork to find me a therapist, and I spent my first session telling my life story. My sob story, as a classmate had once called it. I told her what my last few years of high school had been like, sure to emphasize that it really wasn't that bad because my abuser had never given me a black eye or a broken bone. I told her about my rocky relationship with my stepdad, making clear it was no big deal because kids don't get along with their stepparents all the time. I spent my first session making very sure she knew I was fine.

At the end, she told me how therapy worked and her expectations for our time together. For the next few sessions, I was to come each week prepared to talk about something. It didn't have to be related to my abuse or home life but showing up empty-voiced was not an option. She made it clear I was not renting a friend with our appointments. I was there to learn, heal, and do the work. She also told me therapy was a lot like giving yourself a root canal with a spoon.

I left her office determined to come up with my worst abuse memory. I needed to shock her next week. I believed back then that I needed to earn the right to be called a survivor. If the experience wasn't horrific, it wasn't abuse. It was just something that happened. I opened my second session with what I believed was the worst thing that had been done to me. I was graphic, even explicit as I spoke. The words flowed easily but I felt completely disconnected from the horror I was recounting. It was as though I was talking about something that had happened to someone else. My logical brain knew it was awful, but my emotional brain couldn't connect that truth to a feeling. I was numb. I believed then that I would always be. In many ways, numb was safer because feeling was just so hard.

Near the end of my third session, after dutifully sharing yet another horror story in my quest to prove I was worthy of therapy, she interrupted to ask what feelings were coming up when I talked. I told her the truth. None. She leaned forward, hands clasped in front of her, elbows on her knees and said, "Sit with it for a moment. Tell me what you feel."

We sat in silence. Her looking at me with a patient, focused gaze. Me looking at the picture above her head, the closed files on her desk, the clock on the side table next to her chair. Anywhere but at her. "Embarrassed," I finally said.

"Embarrassed? Why?"

"Because I was already the bad kid of the family. Now I'm the broken fucked up one who embarrassed everyone, too."

"How did you embarrass your family?"

"Because I let this happen. I didn't know what to do so I didn't do anything. The other day I was in a bad mood over it all and my stepdad told me I needed to consider how this affected everyone else. He said it wasn't just about me. He grew up there and now I'm the center of all the gossip. He hates it."

"My sister gets asked about stupid lies and rumors all the time at school," I continued. "Everyone—even my family—treats me different now. They all kind of avoid me. Even more than they did when I was just the bad kid of the house. I hate it."

My voice wandered off, and I went back to avoiding eye contact for the rest of the session. But that day was a breakthrough. It was the first time I'd allowed myself to feel anything but numb or angry. I was honestly surprised I even could feel since I thought for sure I was broken. My therapist diagnosed me with severe CPTSD, or Complex Post Traumatic Stress Disorder. It's odd to admit, but hearing her talk so somberly and clinically about my mental health felt validating. Someone finally looked at me and my experiences and saw an eighteen-year-old who needed support, not a bad kid who got what she deserved.

I worked with her for three years straight and don't think I ever cried during a session. My focus in those early healing days was on the need to be "normal", and a deep desire for my story to be forgotten about. I was tired of standing out. Tired of people gossiping about me while trying to figure out what stories were real, and which were a twisted game of telephone. I was done being the weird outcast. I wasn't sure what normal felt like, all I knew is how I felt was not it. Mostly, though, I just wanted it all to go away so I could stop being embarrassed to exist.

During the early months of my treatment, my therapist tried hard to get me to consider going to group sessions. I refused because my shame was too deep to share with a group of strangers, regardless of shared experiences. She tried to explain that I would find power and strength, or even courage and healing, in knowing that I'm not alone. She told me repeatedly that I had nothing to apologize for or be embarrassed about. She was right, of course, but I wasn't in a place to believe it back then.

Healing did eventually become a bit of an obsession, though. I believed if I learned enough, worked hard enough, I'd eventually reach the glorious nirvana known as "done". In my mind, I likened it to schoolwork. Do the work, get the grade, move on. One of the most impactful things my therapist said to me was if I did the work now, when the pain was fresh, I wouldn't have to feel it again later. That stuck with me because never feeling this way again sounded amazing. And thanks to her, I didn't run from the hard stuff.

She worked diligently to get me to connect to what my feelings were telling me, and to start tuning in to my inner voice. Without fail, every time I shared a story and said I could hear her guidance when I thought or did or felt something, she'd stop me to say it was my own inner voice speaking out, not hers. She encouraged me to listen to it and stay attuned. Our work together provided the first set of tools that helped me navigate the shame and the small-town busybodies who felt entitled to my story. Because of her, I learned boundaries and that I have the right to say no.

She was patient but intent, always challenging me to ask myself hard questions and look at my experiences through different lenses. When I was feeling sorry for myself, she would tell me I could have today for self-pity but tomorrow I needed a plan. Our focus was always on figuring out what actions could I take today, tomorrow, and the next day to get myself to a better place. Feel what you feel when you feel it, but don't get stuck. That was her advice, and it's how I eventually made my way through.

Consent

I started cosmetology school in 1989, right around the time I started therapy. I'd tried community college after graduation, but only lasted one quarter. I'd enrolled because I thought I was supposed to and quickly realized I wasn't ready. The fallout from high school was still front and center of my everyday life. It was the only thing I could focus on, no matter how hard I tried to ignore it and act like every other young girl. But I'd always loved hair and makeup, and I'd heard cosmetologists made good money, so after taking a few months off to just be, I enrolled in a ten-month program.

I gave up my apartment, the one I'd almost been killed in, and moved home so I could afford to attend. To pay the few bills I still had left, I took a job as a hostess in a Mexican restaurant near school. The hours worked perfect with classes and most importantly, between work and school I was busy enough to not have to be home very often. Despite sleeping at home again, I was largely away from small town hell and finally learning to live. I felt happy and I especially treasured the new friendships I was forming at work. After surviving high school and my home life, it was such a relief to meet new people who had no idea who I was beyond the person they saw. I loved it.

The young man who sexually assaulted me was one of my coworkers. He had a dangerous smile and bright blue eyes. He was tall, blonde, confident, a little cocky, and I couldn't look away. We had been working together a few months, talking during and after most shifts. I was so awkward. I hung on his every word, but I was certain he had no interest beyond casual conversation. He told me he lived with his girlfriend, but they were basically broken up. In fact, they didn't even sleep in the same room. They only lived together because they couldn't get out of their lease. We flirted a little now and then. I was so starved for attention that it never occurred to me to question anything he said. We were friends. Why would he lie?

One night, he invited me to his place. He said his girlfriend was out of town, so he was having friends over to hang out after work. I couldn't figure out if he liked me or was just including me because we worked together. I didn't care. I got to his apartment and saw a small group of people sitting on the floor of the living room playing drinking games and talking. They were all very welcoming, inviting me to join. I was nineteen and didn't drink. I certainly had no idea how to play whatever drinking game they were playing, but I was determined to fit in. Besides, participating meant I got to sit next to him.

I don't remember much about the game other than I lost and drank the better part of three beers in a short amount of time. I quickly started feeling the effects of the alcohol. He noticed and said I needed to lie down. He led me to his room and helped me into his waterbed, fully clothed save for my shoes.

"Is this your girlfriend's?" I remember asking when I saw the other bedroom on my way to his. I don't remember his answer. He left a nightlight on and told me to get some sleep before shutting the door.

I remember lying there, alone, curled into the fetal position, praying everything – including the damn waterbed – would stop moving. The next thing I remember is waking up to him having sex with me. I was half-dressed, shirt and bra still on, underwear and jeans shoved down, bunched around one ankle.

I was disoriented. The room was still spinning. The nightlight was still on. I was on the same side of the bed where he'd left me earlier. I stared at the ceiling with the same detachment that saw me through high school. My body was not my own. I'd return when it was over, but for now this was one more thing I had to endure. When he was done, he told me I'd initiated it.

He stopped speaking to me after that night. The girlfriend came back from wherever she had been. Gossip made the rounds that they were moving to a new place together, happier than ever. We all moved on with our lives like nothing ever happened.

I didn't recognize his actions as inappropriate back then. It didn't even hit my radar that what happened was an assault, despite it being the very definition of a date rape. The world was different in 1989. So was I. My nineteen-year-old body still defaulted to detachment and dissociation anytime something felt uncertain or uncomfortable. So, in truth, the encounter registered as far more normal than it should. I didn't know enough then to realize that being passed out meant I was unable to consent. He'd robbed me of the opportunity to say no. Or yes.

In 1989, I had barely started fighting the lifelong conditioning about sex and sexuality that required only feelings of shame, regardless of the circumstances. So instead of treating myself kindly in the aftermath of yet another act of abuse, I existed solely on fresh waves of humiliation. I'd believed the lies about the girlfriend and I had a crush on him. I knew that if he'd asked, I'd have said yes. That was enough for me to be disgusted with myself.

Life moved on, though, and I tucked the memory away, at times even forgetting about it altogether. Nearly thirty years later, I saw his name in a newspaper article about a murder trial. That's when I found out he'd become a respected homicide detective. That's also when all the memories came rushing back. They demanded to be seen, to be processed, through the lens of what I know now, and all the work I've done to get here.

I was able to give nineteen-year-old me the grace that was unavailable then. It didn't matter than I liked him. It didn't matter that I would have said yes if he'd asked. It didn't matter that I drank or that I passed out in his bed or that I didn't stop him when I woke up and realized what was happening. None of that mattered in the slightest. What mattered was that I was not asked. What mattered was that my agency over my body was taken away again. At a time when I was barely recovering from it happening the first time. I gave myself permission to put the responsibility squarely on the shoulders of the young man who didn't give me the chance to say no.

Strangely, I felt no anger toward him. None. I'm long past it, and honestly don't have the energy to carry the negativity it would require. When I think about it now, I think about the lost and struggling young woman I used to be. I choose to channel my energy toward giving her the deep empathy and compassion she deserves.

Promiscuity and Unavailable Men

I was promiscuous for about two years in my early twenties. It was fun. I learned a lot about sex, about people,
and about myself. I discovered the power that comes from
sexuality. I loved the confidence of being a young woman
who no longer had to hold her head down in shame every
time someone found her attractive. I have never regretted
it. Not once. Not when my mom called me a slut and said
she'd never take a blood transfusion from me because she
didn't want to catch anything. And not when my stepdad
said I'd been trained better and called me a whore.

After the promiscuous years, I found that I tended to
gravitate toward unavailable men. Unavailable emotionally. Physically. Geographically. Sometimes, I was even
stupid enough to believe the ones who were already in
a relationship really meant it when they said how bad

things were at home and how different they felt when talking to me. Maybe it was daddy issues. Maybe it was insecurity. Maybe it was the acting out of a damaged woman. Maybe a combination of all three.

Whatever it was at its core, being drawn to unavailable men was a pattern I didn't have the self-awareness or courage to recognize until my late forties. Before then, I believed it was equal parts bad luck and all I deserved.

Unwanted, unimportant little girls do not believe they have the right to be selective about who wants them. What we want is far less important than the fact that someone wants us. We need to shut up and be grateful. It does not occur to us that we have the right to wait for someone who can give us what we need. It does not occur to us that we are worth more. It does not occur to us that a life alone is better than what we have been accepting so far. Not until we decide to dig in and do the work.

In truth, unavailable men were safe. I never had to worry about them waking up one day to realize loving me was a mistake, because they would never be around long enough to know the real me. I never had to worry they'd leave me as soon as I got vulnerable because the dynamics were never equal, and I rarely let them in. Rejection and abandonment are easier to swallow from people who have never seen you with your guard down.

Apart from the emotional safeguards of being involved with the unavailable, there is also the seductive, romanticized, sexy side of feeling wanted by someone who is not *supposed* to want you. Truthfully, I believed no one was ever supposed to want me, so the fact that someone spent time thinking about me was like heroin to my attention-craving soul.

I used to believe I was invisible. That once out of sight, no one gave me a second thought. I believed that to be especially true for men. To have someone reach out of the blue to say I was on their mind was a high like no other. To have someone find me attractive was intoxicating. Me, the little girl no one was proud to claim as their own grew into someone people thought about. That felt close enough to love. It was what I thought I needed. I chased it, clung to it, until I learned better.

PART II: DISCOVERY

But in the end truth will out.
— Shakespeare

No Honor in Misery

I started working with my second therapist in 1999, shortly after my first divorce. Our work helped me process the feelings of guilt and shame that came from ending my marriage, while also supporting my continued journey to heal from my trauma. She re-diagnosed my CPTSD along with an anxiety disorder that developed in the decade since I first sought treatment. My therapist had a quiet, calm, nurturing style that made me feel safe and comfortable from the start. She was also very no nonsense and held me accountable at every step.

Being fresh out of a marriage after a lifetime of being unable to trust love, I was emotionally raw and very fix-ated on guarantees. I was determined to fix myself com-pletely so I would never have to go through the pain of a divorce again. My therapist worked tirelessly to get me to understand that even people without a history of trauma struggle with certainty and the concept of forever. I was still convinced I was broken, and that other people didn't struggle with basic emotional connection the way I did. She worked to help me see that being able to leave, being able to change, and being able to grow was a gift and a skill. My second therapist is the one who told me it was okay to leave a relationship if I, or the other person, became someone else. She taught me there is no honor in misery and there is no victory in staying simply because you swore never to leave. I learned from her that growth sometimes leads people apart and that even the best matches come with no guarantees.

I remember her as the first person to really push me to figure out who I am and what I like. Her constant, supportive encouragement allowed me to take my first steps in defining myself by my own standards instead of feeling like a failure trying to live up to someone else's. She taught me that pain and healing were not competitive sports. I wasn't worth less, and my suffering wasn't less important, simply because someone else may have struggled more or differently.

I learned from my first therapist that there were no shortcuts and that the only way out to was to do the work. My second taught me that deep healing and growth happens in the quiet times. Even when I felt stagnant and bored, convinced I was stuck at a dead end, my subconscious was still working hard.

My work with her kept me moving forward at a time when all I wanted was to curl up and retreat.

Loving Narcissists

One of the most heartbreaking epiphanies of my life came the day I realized the reason I had so much trouble choosing healthy relationships wasn't only because of a lifetime of complicated daddy issues. It was also, and no less, from being raised in a lie by a narcissistic mother. I don't blame her anymore, because I'm certain she was merely repeating what she'd learned in her own life, but from a young age, chaos, instability, and living slightly on edge is what felt like home. Emotional discomfort was comforting because it was familiar, and constantly needing to earn love and prove my worthiness felt normal.

Gaslighting was a regular part of my life for so long that as an adult I had no idea how to function in a relationship with someone who wasn't always rewriting facts or history to suit their needs. Growing up, I didn't have the vocabulary to describe what was happening, or even the ability to understand the power of gaslighting and narcissism. I didn't even know there was a name for what I experienced, partly because I had no idea anything different existed. What I did know was that my mom's version of events was often inconsistent with my memory. It was rarely the same from one retelling to the next, and she was always furious when I tried to call her on it. I also knew she seemed to care an awful lot about how others saw her and her parenting. What others thought about us and our family was far more important than how her kids felt. Back then, however, I had no way of knowing that this didn't happen in all families. I thought it was normal, if incredibly frustrating.

When I later graduated to loving, then marrying, a narcissist, I found myself in the same familiar emotionally uncomfortable space that felt like home. I chose someone determined to keep my life emotionally unsteady. Having already been through one divorce, I was determined to avoid another at any and all cost. This made me the perfect mate for someone disinterested in a balanced and loving partnership. I was willing to jump through hoops to earn love but otherwise fly under the radar to avoid making waves. I minimized my needs, my wants, and my accomplishments. I was always afraid of appearing to overshadow, or of seeming "too much." In time, I came to accept my husband's truth that everything would be fine if I were just somehow better.

I lived on edge, constantly walking a very narrow tightrope to keep him happy. I worked hard to make myself more accepting, more accommodating, less demanding, less needy. I genuinely believed that I could carry the relationship alone and that he didn't need to do anything. In fact, I believed it was my *job* since I was clearly the broken one and he had it all together. Obviously, he loved me enough to want me to get better, so pointing out what I'd done wrong or what I needed to fix was just him trying to help. And he loved me enough to want me to know exactly why I was always wrong. I lost years of my life waiting for the day he would finally accept and appreciate me. For the day when I'd done enough work to be able to surrender and trust and just feel loved. That day never came.

One time, after an argument just a few months into our relationship, he called me a nasty name as he hung up the phone. I called back and was trying to hold him accountable when he said, "I don't know what you think you heard" then hung up on me again. I heard it. I knew I heard it. He knew I heard it. His response to getting caught was to deflect, deny, to rewrite the truth, and to make me question my own experience, feelings, and memory. But what I remember most about that day is not anger, or sadness that the man who claimed to love me called me a horrible name then lied about it. No, what I remember is feeling strong and empowered.

That's where I was in my healing journey. Instead of walking away from someone who would talk to me like that and call it love, I was proud of myself for having the courage to speak up. It had taken a lifetime to feel that strong. I felt like I used my voice and demanded respect, which was so unlike me. It was one of the most validating conversations of our relationship because it showed me how far I'd come. I can look back now and see how far I still had to go, but at the time, it felt like a huge victory.

Sadly, I didn't ask myself the deeper question of why I would choose to stay and love him. That thought was nowhere near my realm of consciousness. The idea that someone calling me a nasty name could—and should— be enough to end a relationship never crossed my mind. I believed then that all relationships came with a bit of mistreatment. Trusting that I could love myself enough to wait to be treated with kindness, even during disagreements, was something I didn't even know to imagine.

I believed if I called it out every time, and if I stated my boundary over and over (and over and over) again, he would respect me. Eventually, he would love me the way I wanted to be loved. I just knew it. All I had to do was be patient and keep asking him to be nice.

That didn't happen, of course, and in time the dark truth of his personality took hold. I grew to distrust acts of kindness because they generally hid an ulterior motive or more disrespectful behavior. I smiled and acted my part through grand gestures of love and devotion that played out in front of an audience, but did not reflect what was happening at home. Behind closed doors I lived in a constant state of insecurity and anxiety, wondering if today was when it would all fall apart. Or, more accurately, if today was when I would decide I couldn't take it anymore.

I rarely worried that he'd leave, which honestly felt like another victory for the little girl constantly terrified of being abandoned. I believed he'd stay, live his life how he wanted, and do everything in his power to make mine miserable whenever it suited him. Truthfully, part of what I fought against internally for so long, and a key piece of what made me stay, was the fear and shame of failing at yet another marriage. The very idea of it was horrifying. That self-torture kept me in it every bit as much as the trauma bond.

Eventually I did leave, but not without staying long enough to add some deep emotional scars to the ones I was already carrying. The lasting effects of surviving yet another narcissistic relationship still show up, even all these years later. I am overly cautious in my private life. I am a rule-follower because clear guidelines and expectations give me certainty. I prefer living alone because it's emotionally safe and I never want to walk on eggshells in my home again. I like structure and routine, chase stability, hate surprises, and always need to know what's happening next.

I will *never* like being teased because life with a narcissist means being told to "lighten up," "get a sense of humor," or "learn to take a joke," every time a comment goes too far, which is pretty much all the time. Narcissists use teasing to mask their cruelty and to convince you it's socially acceptable. They need you to believe that the problem is you, not them. I have no patience for practical jokes or someone who thinks trying to scare me is funny. It triggers deep feelings of betrayal that I won't have in my world again.

I save texts, emails, screenshots, even receipts. Anything to show that someone said what I remember them saying, or that what I read is really what was written. I don't do these things because I am spiteful or petty. I do it because I have had to relearn to trust myself and documentation helps me stand firm in what I know for sure.

The emotional foundation for people raised by a narcissist is a house of cards threatened by a summer breeze. It is clear the whole thing will crumble at any moment, but you try your best to protect it anyway. I've come to see it as a pattern repeated in my relationships. I choose someone who makes me feel they are doing me a favor in loving and choosing me. I contort myself into someone unrecognizable trying to hold that love while they keep me on edge by constantly changing the expectations. I then realize I can't be the person being with them has turned me into, so I leave. My relationships were the house of cards. The legacy of being raised by a narcissist is the breeze. The hope of a different outcome is me trying to protect it anyway.

Motherhood

Had anyone asked the teen and young adult me if I someday wanted kids, the answer would have been a resounding no. I was raised as the oldest of five, and by the time I graduated from high school I'd already spent years taking care of babies. I knew I did not want to be responsible for anyone else. That's not to say I was passionately anti-motherhood. I wasn't. It just honestly held no interest. Instead, I wanted my independence. I had dreams of traveling the world, and of writing books. I wanted to see new things and meet new people and fall in love and be free. I wanted to escape my life and create something magical. I wanted something different.

My first pregnancy caught me by surprise. My wild days were behind me, barely, and I was gradually shifting toward a mellower life. I was twenty-five and working two jobs while trying to finish my degree. It didn't occur to me that the reason for my exhaustion, weight loss, and nausea was my uterus turning into a home. I thought it was stress. Or trying to survive on a diet of junk food and caffeine. Or maybe the flu.

It took some time to start thinking of myself as someone's mom. I'd barely gotten used to living for me, and suddenly I was living for two. It rightfully changed everything, and demanded a shift in perspective that took a minute to fully understand. My determination to be in control of my life was magnified, but somehow looked different. It wasn't about defiantly being able to do whatever whenever and answering to no one. Now it was about making sure I had choices. It was about making sure I could take care of myself as well as any future children.

I didn't know who or how I'd be as a parent. The only thing I knew for sure was that I never wanted my child to spend a second of their life feeling the way I did. That core truth provided the focus I needed to figure out the rest. By the time I gave birth to my son, I was wildly in love and confident that I could do it right. When his brother arrived less than two years later, I was consumed by motherhood and my love for them. I was present. I was engaged. I was connected. They were my everything.

As they grew, so did I. We navigated life's ups and downs, our collective stubborn personalities, the drama of teenage defiance, and all the moments before, after, and in between, together. My happiest moments are with them. The first time I felt pure joy was with them. The pictures I love most feature their smiling faces next to mine.

Choosing to support them unconditionally, making sure they've always known the only side I'm ever on is theirs, was as much for me as them. Forcing myself to stand back while they navigated their own hard times, when all I wanted to do was fix it, was brutal. Harder than just about anything else I've ever done. But watch-

ing them grow, having an impact on the men they've become, has been the great honor of my life.

That's not to say I was the perfect mom. I absolutely
wasn't. I was frustrated and impatient at times they deserved patience and calm. I occasionally let my own stuff
cloud my judgement instead of focusing solely on present
facts and circumstances. And sometimes I blindly trusted
the sincere pleas and mischievous eyes that led to perfectly age-appropriate trouble.

What I know for sure is that I am the perfect mom for
my kids. And if I'm being really honest, I'm not sure I'd
do motherhood well with any others. But for the two souls
I was entrusted with guiding, no one could have raised
them better or loved them more.

Messenger

Growing up in a trailer in the middle of nowhere didn't lend itself to great hope. I had no career ambition, no plans beyond maybe going to community college, one day, eventually. But I liked reading and learning, and I loved stories set in exotic foreign lands. I always dreamed of traveling, even though I was never sure how I could make it happen. For a time, I was fixated on becoming a game show contestant so I could win a once-in-a-lifetime trip during the showcase showdown.

A lot changed in my life after the years in the trailer, but my love of and fascination with travel never did. In the late fall of 2012, I was depressed and feeling unsettled while waiting for my second divorce to become final. I knew I needed to get away, ideally to someplace that required a passport stamp, but I was a little anxious about doing international travel alone. Most of my travel up until then had been going on vacation with husbands, a group of girlfriends, or on trips with the kids. Months earlier, my ex and I had planned to take a Mediterranean cruise. When I called to cancel, I found out the deposit was fully refundable. Hearing that felt like permission to do something for myself. The day I got my money back, I booked a weeklong tour of Prague and Budapest.

I chose a tour for a couple of reasons. First, it would nudge me to socialize and be around people, and second, it meant all the logistics were handled. The thought of having to coordinate hotels, the travel between cities, and all activities or sightseeing felt a little overwhelming considering everything else I was navigating at the time. I did pay extra for a private room, though, because wherever I am, I am still an introvert and I need time alone to recharge.

I intentionally did no research on either city other than a cursory review of the itinerary. I'd used the tour company before, so I chose to trust them and let the adventure unfold. I was excited but a little lonely on the flight to Amsterdam. I wasn't used to being without a travel companion, so having no one to share anything with was an adjustment. I'd bought a new journal specifically for the trip and spent time between free movies filling up pages.

Landing in Amsterdam's Schiphol Airport was a homecoming. A decade earlier, it had been the layover stop on my first European trip, and being there again felt like a sign from the universe that my soul is returning to where it's supposed to be. It's also one of my favorite airports. Beautiful people everywhere. Flight crews in their blue KLM Royal Dutch Airlines uniforms looking like they just stepped out of a 1960s ad campaign. Nearly everyone spoke at least a little English, which helps someone like me who speaks nothing else. I was tired from the overnight flight, but quickly reenergized after making it through customs, proudly bearing a passport stamp approving my entry into the EU.

After a short layover, I boarded my flight to Prague. Seated next to me was a fellow American who said he was headed to the Czech Republic on business. We shared travel stories, his more exciting than mine. The flight was starting its descent when I saw snow. My seatmate saw it, too, and told me it was supposed to be cold for the next week. I packed for crisp end of October weather, not winter. I was going to freeze.

We landed and I was instantly overwhelmed. I couldn't read the signs. Nothing looked to be open. It seemed like everyone knew where to go while I stood frozen, staring up, trying to find baggage claim. The rush of energy I felt when I'd landed in Amsterdam had faded, and I was suddenly exhausted. In the back of my mind, I could hear a little voice saying I had no business thinking I was capable of traveling alone.

I took a deep breath, shook off the negative voice, and followed the crowd. To my surprise, a young man dressed casually in jeans and wearing a jacket with a hotel logo was waiting near the baggage carousel bearing a sign with my name. I'd forgotten I'd taken the hotel up on their offer of a driver. He ushered me to a black Audi then we were on our way as he navigated the twists and turns of Prague's roads before arriving in Old Town.

I loved everything about both Prague and Budapest. The people were friendly and welcoming, excited to show us the beauty of their cities. The streets felt safe, even when I was walking alone in the evening. One of my favorite memories is walking the town squares in brisk late fall weather with a paper cup of spiced mulled wine purchased from a street market. But what I remember most about that trip is a feeling of hope, and surrender. Every morning while getting ready to explore, I would play some

Adele and allow myself to feel hope. The change of scenery alone was proof that a whole world of happiness existed outside of my misery. All I had to do was surrender and let it unfold.

Prague also introduced me to a messenger sent straight from the universe. One of the women on the tour was traveling with her young adult daughter. They were kind enough to allow me to tag along on some of their sightseeing. We had the best talks about life and divorce and relationships. She was divorced, had raised her kids mostly alone, and was now in what she called the healthiest relationship of her life. During dinner one night, she looked at me and said, "happiness is out there. But you have to believe you deserve it."

Message received.

Being in a new place, away from the routines of daily life, brought clarity. I began to feel empowered. Inspired. A few days in Prague and Budapest, and meeting a messenger, gave me the courage to believe in a future full of happiness. I flew home ten days later, having found my smile. My friends and I came to call it my *Eat Pray Love* trip. I didn't find love in Bali with a kind Brazilian man or spend more than a few minutes meditating, and I certainly didn't become fluent in Italian. But I did come back to life.

Epiphany: January 2013

I don't remember the exact date, but I know where I was the second my brain landed on the truth. I was driving home from work, passing a park near the elementary school my kids once attended. I'd had a few rough months and was working through a bit of an emotional hangover. My second divorce was nearly final after a yearlong battle over nothing since I'd willingly given him everything just to be free. I was still digging out of the financial black hole created as part of his scorched earth approach to destroying my life. And I was working with my therapist to try to figure out how I ended up doing yet another life rebuild at forty-two.

It wasn't one specific thing that made me question everything. Rather, it was a series of smaller things— little truths, lingering questions—popping up unbidden, growing more and more insistent, and demanding to be acknowledged.

My sister Erica had recently posted a picture with our dad, Gene, on Facebook. I hadn't seen him in person for years, and I hadn't seen him side by side with her in even more. Their resemblance was unmistakable. Same smile, same eyes, same general look. Around that time, I saw a cousin at the grocery store. I remember looking at her thinking the similarities to my sister, my other cousins, my aunt, and my dad were plain as day. Not me, though. I saw nothing of myself in their faces. Why didn't I look like my family?

Watching my kids grow over the years, I could always see they were a perfect blend of their dad and me. When with me, people would say they looked like me. The same thing happened when they were with their dad. When we were all together, there was no mistaking their genetics.

But me? The older I got, the less I looked like anyone – other than the lifelong likeness to my mom, and even that was fading with time. Why didn't I look like anyone else? Wasn't it weird that everyone I knew looked at least a little like both of their parents, while I only looked like one?

Looking at that Facebook post and feeling nothing had made me wonder again why I never felt connected to him. Why I never felt a father-daughter bond. My sister clearly did. In fact, she felt it so strongly that she maintained a relationship with him even after everything he'd done to Mom and to us. For me, it was frightfully easy to walk away and never look back. It honestly made me wonder if I was heartless because I barely felt that deep parental connection to my mom, and she was the parent who had always been there.

The questions kept rushing at me:

Why is it so hard for me to form emotional connections to people?

If I don't feel connected to my own father or to my extended family, am I capable of love at all?

How can I trust the love I have for my siblings or my closest friends, no matter how strong it feels?

Why do I struggle so much with men and relationships?

What the hell is wrong with me that this is my life?

For some reason, that night, I couldn't shake the questions. Every time I dismissed one, another popped up. I knew I was emotionally exhausted from my divorce, so I tried to tell myself my brain was doing its usual overthinking. Nothing to see here, folks, just the crazy lady trying to make sense of shit that does not make sense. Maybe I really was just losing my mind. The questions kept coming, though, demanding I pay attention. And, suddenly, there it was. The only truth that fit. One I couldn't believe had taken me so long to see.

He's not my dad.

Oh, my God. That's it. That's why I don't look like him. That's why I

don't look like my sister. That's why I
don't look like anyone on his side of the
family. That's why I have no emotion
about him.

I remember one clear feeling from the rest of that drive home: relief. I felt genuine, absolute relief. I wasn't related to the asshole who used to beat my mom. I shared no blood with the kind of monster who walks away from his children without a second thought. He is not mine. I do not have to claim him. I never have to see him again.

A strange and uneasy peace came over me in the days that followed. Uneasy because it felt like the beginning of something, every bit as much as the end. Strange because somewhere inside I believed I'd always known. My physical, emotional, and spiritual selves had been rejecting this man my whole life. It just took decades to land on a why that wasn't steeped in blame and self-loathing. Once I did, everything came into focus.

I did nothing with my epiphany at the time. I needed to keep it hidden and safe while I processed and figured out what to do next.

New Year's Eve: 2015

I've been called nosy, a busybody, detective, a dog with a bone. In truth, I've been called all kinds of things by people eager to reduce my fear of lies to a character defect. My closest circle of friends and family, the ones who have stuck with me through everything, have always understood why. They know that my obsession with the truth and aversion to secrets comes from a lifetime of being fed stories that almost invariably unraveled when inspected closely. All I've ever wanted was to know that the people I trusted weren't keeping secrets or telling lies, especially the kinds of lies that destroy a child's sense of stability and a woman's belief that anything will ever really be okay.

By the time Mom and I met for breakfast that New Year's Eve morning, I'd had my suspicions about my dad for a couple of years. More accurately, I'd known the truth in my heart for a couple of years. I'd even worked up the courage to ask the question more than once. The answers were always vague and unclear stories that changed with every new question, or new piece of information independently uncovered. Lies on top of lies. I had no doubt the truth was being kept from me, but I needed proof before I could call it out. It had to be something objective and irrefutable, and something decidedly more tangible than what I felt in my soul the second my subconscious forced me to take a step back and see the truth.

So, for two full years I'd waited. I finally got my proof in the form of a color-coded pie chart courtesy of Ancestry. com. Erica and I had signed up to find out about our heritage. We'd both always wanted to know if we were Irish or English or German or whatever. Unsurprisingly, when we were growing up Mom always found ways to avoid the question any time we'd asked. We both saw Ancestry. com as our chance to get some answers. What Erica didn't know was that I had an ulterior motive and was secretly looking for confirmation that we weren't full siblings.

I wanted to be stunned the day I got my results. I wanted to feel validated. I wanted to feel something. What I felt instead was nothing.

My lack of emotion was sad, but not surprising. I have always operated on autopilot when dealing with emotionally heavy or stressful times. It's my go-to coping mechanism. I go into survival mode, focusing on nothing more than getting through. The emotional processing comes later. Always later.

I waited a few months before telling anyone other than my brother, Steven. I don't know why, other than I wasn't ready for conversations I knew would be difficult. It wasn't my fault that this secret had been kept from me, but that didn't stop me from feeling guilty and ashamed for daring to look deeper. But now I had the truth, and the bad kid of the family was about to stir up trouble. After the usual hectic madness of the holidays, I reached out to Mom. I wanted to start the new year free of secrets and lies, hoping to finally feel some peace.

Mom and I met mid-morning. She looked so excited. She was happy to be asked to breakfast by the daughter she'd been mostly estranged from for the better part of thirty years. We ordered, though I had no appetite, and then made casual small talk while we waited. I had butterflies in my stomach, but I was determined to calmly present my case and finally get some answers. I'd even practiced what I intended to say and how I would handle what I was sure would be her attempts at deflection or denial. By this time, I knew about gaslighting, and I knew how good she was at it.

"Mom," I said, "Erica and I did Ancestry.com a few months ago. I know we're half-sisters."

I watched the color drain from her face. I watched her start to tremble. I felt the familiar pangs of guilt and shame. Once again, I felt like the bad kid asking questions and pushing back instead of blindly and obediently accepting. I leaned toward her in anticipation, convinced she was about to tell me my birth father's name, or maybe even the story behind the lies.

"Then whose are you?"

Excuse me? What the fuck? I thought to myself, completely caught off guard. This was not at all what I had expected.

"I don't know, Mom," I replied, "I was hoping you'd tell me."

She was shaking when she reached for my hands and said, "Honey, I was raped."

She told me about being newly married and her husband not picking her up from her shift at the truck stop diner where she worked. She told me she waited for a couple of hours before accepting a ride home from an unknown customer. She told me a story that ended with a sexual assault.

Oh, my God. I'm a rape baby? Again, whatever I thought I had prepared myself for, it wasn't this.

I had done the math and I knew I was conceived during the holidays. I expected a story about a Christmas or New Year's Eve party that got out of control. Or maybe an affair. It was 1969, after all. Free love and all that, right?

"Honey, I had no idea you weren't Gene's," she swore with still-shaking hands and a plaintive voice, imploring me to believe her. "I don't know who the guy was. I never saw him again after that." She looked so fragile. She was trembling when I asked for a name, a description, any detail that could help me create an image in my head of who he was and who I am.

I listened with a newfound compassion. I tried to put myself in the shoes of a barely educated, twenty-year-old diner waitress in 1969. A different time. A different generation. A world where women had much less of a voice, and choice, than they do now. I was devastated watching her regress before my eyes, turning into a broken young woman reliving pain.

I felt so guilty. I'd broken my mother. How dare I dig up the past and force her to share her trauma in the name of my selfish need for the truth? What kind of ungrateful child traumatizes her mother and turns her back into a victim knowing she is incapable of processing a single emotion?

I heard my own voice crack from holding back tears as I asked, "do you see me differently now?" She said no and asked the same question of me through tears of her own. I gave the same answer.

I knew we'd made a breakthrough. With the truth finally out, we could begin to heal a lifetime of estrangement. Oh, the hope and love I had in those brief moments before the broken woman I was listening to morphed back into the woman I had always known.

"Don't tell the family," she said finally. "Who else knows?"

There it was. Damage control.

That's when I knew we would never be healed. I didn't matter. My truth didn't matter. The horrible story she'd just told me – and its impact – didn't matter. What mattered to her was who knew and how to keep anyone else from finding out. Once again, I was shown that my very existence was a source of shame and a burden to the people who were supposed to love me.

I told her that my inner circle knew because they'd been on the journey with me long before I knew it ended with a sexual assault and conception in a pickup.

"Okay," she said anxiously, "but don't tell anyone else. And delete your profile so no one can find out."

"I'll never lead with it, Mom, but I won't lie and I'm not taking on any shame. It's my story and my truth to share. I get to decide who I tell, not you."

For the first time, I refused to accept shame or continue to apologize for the crime of existing. If Mom felt ashamed, she could carry that on her own. If she needed to process her trauma, that was her work to do. Not mine.

She was visibly disappointed and tried hard to negotiate. In the end, what calmed her down was me saying I had no plans to broadcast the news and had little to no contact with the extended family she was so worried about. I also had to promise not to tell the rest of my siblings.

I left breakfast feeling raw and shaken. I drove aimlessly for a while, unsure where to go or what to think. I was happy to finally have some answers, but wasn't sure what to do with them because they led to so many new questions. None of it lined up with anything I'd prepared myself to hear. I also felt my usual hodgepodge of mixed feelings about Mom. Deep compassion for 1969 her blended with lifelong frustration and lingering resentment toward modern-day her.

Her attempt at manipulation and control caught me off guard, even though it shouldn't have. Who cares if people find out? Why was it so wrong to want to know the truth? Why do I always feel like a piece of her is ashamed of me? Why do other people's opinions matter more than my feelings? It's something I have never understood about her and I felt more angry than usual about it that day.

I eventually found myself at Target, wandering like a zombie and filling my cart with assorted oddities I definitely did not need. I texted brief updates to the handful of friends who knew about breakfast but mostly pushed my cart up and down the aisles in a daze. Mom didn't call or text to see how I was doing, but I checked on her a few hours later. She said she was okay and that she loved me. I encouraged her to talk to someone about all the feelings this was bound to stir up. She promised she would.

It didn't occur to me to be upset that she wasn't asking about my feelings. Honestly, it's not something she did under the most normal of circumstances, and the times she tried felt less like authentic emotional engagement and more like check-the-box efforts. I knew her, and I knew her limits. Which meant I knew she'd do her best to never talk about this again. Unless it suited her, or unless she needed to do damage control.

In the weeks that followed, I found that my heart softened and hardened toward her, depending on the feelings of the day. I checked on her more than usual and repeatedly said I hoped she was talking to someone. When I was feeling bold, I'd ask a few questions to try to make sense of it all. Softball ones, though, not the heavy hitters that were still lurking about. I knew I wasn't ready yet to take on those. Mom did everything in her power to avoid answering no matter what I asked. I could barely get her to engage on the topic for more than a moment before she inevitably went silent or changed the subject.

In time, I gave up. She'd told me all she was willing, or able, to share. I did my best to make peace with the reality of my conception and the fact that I may never know my father's name. "Sometimes we don't get the answers we want," my first therapist used to say. She was right. So, I did my best to move on.

New Orleans

Priestess

New Orleans feels like magic to me. Its history, culture, architecture, lore. My soul is drawn to it the same way I'm drawn to Europe, despite only having visited once back in 1993. I love everything about the city, except maybe the muggy heat. But even that adds to its intoxicating vibe.

In 2017, I was thrilled to get to go back. I was there for a work conference, and it came as no surprise that I fell right back under its spell the second I stepped off the plane. The airport shuttle dropped me at a hotel in the central business district, about a fifteen-minute walk from the French Quarter, where I and a small group of work friends were staying.

Mornings were spent at the conference for seminars and breakout sessions then we explored the city in the afternoon and evenings. We did a city walking tour on our first full day that included a stop at St. Louis Cemetery No. 1, final resting place of Marie Laveau, known as the Voodoo Queen of New Orleans. The next day, we went on an afternoon walking tour of haunted places in the heart of the city that conveniently stopped at Lafitte's Blacksmith Shop Bar, where we had a drink and marveled at everything New Orleans offered.

That night, while I was walking through the French Quarter with one of the women from work, I decided on a whim to get a reading. We turned the corner and chose the next place we saw. I gave my first name to the young man at the entrance, then paid for my thirty-minute appointment in cash. He led us through the courtyard, stopping at a table next to the fountain at its center and asked us to wait until someone came to escort me to the priestess. It was a dark night in mid-June with only the stars and a few strands of lights strung from corner to corner softly brightening the open space.

When my appointment came, I was taken up a staircase to a sparse room with soft low light, red walls, and a small round table in the center with two chairs. The windows were slid open, letting in the warm night breeze. The priestess entered through a side door, arms outstretched, to introduce herself and ask my name. She was clad in a purple and red print dress with dark sandals and wore her hair in long dreadlocks that were starting to gray. Her brown eyes studied mine intently, only breaking their gaze when she looked at my palm.

"How are you here?" She asked, looking shocked as her eyes went back and forth between my outstretched hand and my eyes. "People don't survive the things you've been through."

That caught me off guard. Did she say this to everyone? Or did she really see my story? I smiled nervously but didn't answer.

She gestured for me to sit at the table then began my reading. It started with generalities that could easily apply to anyone. Things like me recently going through a rough time and coming out stronger, and seeing change coming my way.

"What brought you to New Orleans?" She asked.

"I'm here for work."

"You won't be doing that kind of work much longer. You're done with that and will be working for yourself soon."

She was wrong. I liked my job and had no plans for a career change, but I didn't say anything. I had no interest in owning my own business. I liked the stability of corporate life. Seriously, what single mother in her right mind gives up a good, steady job?

Her eyes grew more focused and intent as the minutes passed. Soon enough, she was focused on my energy and started providing details that felt specific to me. One of the things she said repeatedly was, "Why aren't you writing? That's your future. You need to be writing."

I was surprised and didn't know how to react. I had given only my first name at the front desk. At the time, I had no social media presence, so a Facebook or Instagram search before my reading would have turned up nothing. She had no way of knowing writing has always been a lifeline. I loved creative writing in school and have always worked out emotions through journaling. I've also always had a dream of making a living as a writer. It is central to who I am.

She continued to talk about big changes coming to my life and my need to take a risk. We never talked about love or romance or relationships. She didn't tell me that she saw some great love coming my way, or that heartache was on the horizon. Her words focused on me, my life, and who I am.

I didn't talk much since she'd asked very few questions. Honestly, she didn't need to because some people just know things. She looked in my eyes, she stared at my palm, and she shared what she saw. Time and again, though, she circled back to a central message: I'd overcome what I was supposed to overcome. It was time to take a leap and stop looking back.

PART III: NEW BEGINNINGS

No matter how hard the past is,
you can always begin again.
— Jack Kornfield

Connecting
Mind to Body

Within months of my second marriage, I had begun looking for another therapist. Initially, it was for couples
counseling, ostensibly to help us navigate the natural
issues arising from a newly blended family. Unfortunately,
it quickly became obvious that I had married a man who
thought all our problems would be fixed if I simply read his
mind, never questioned anything he did, and, most importantly, had no needs of my own.

Eventually, I started seeing this therapist on my own.
I was determined to make my marriage work, and I was
deeply convinced that if I just worked hard enough, I
could earn back the love that had gotten me to the altar. I
couldn't, of course. Life with a narcissist can never be good.
I had waited years for a chance at a life of love, peace, and
acceptance. I had *worked* to get to a place where I believed

I deserved those things, and then I married a man addicted to chaos and drama. I couldn't see any of this back then because I was too caught up in the trauma bond and the never-ending cycle of lies, empty promises, and emotional abuse. But I am certain my therapist spotted it all right away. In fact, he was the first person to use the word narcissist to describe both my mother and my husband.

Each of my therapists have brought different tools and styles to our work together. This therapist spent a lot of time teaching me to pay attention to my body language as a clue to my subconscious, and my truth. I had spent so many years trying to read the minds of my partners and meet their every need that I'd forgotten to be aware of my own needs, my own thoughts, and my own feelings.

Over time, I learned to observe how I sat and spoke when trying to convince myself (or anyone else) that my relationship was salvageable. I was small and closed off, trying to take as little space as possible. My shoulders were up at my ears, but somehow still slumped and turned inward. My arms were crossed protectively over my chest, my heart, and I regularly rubbed my hands together to self-soothe. My voice carried an edge, a twinge of defensive vigilance, always.

My therapist helped me see that my traumas were resurfacing because I married someone who had meticulously learned my secrets – my pain – for the sole purpose of using it against me. I was heartbroken the day I realized I'd committed my life to a man who delighted in betraying my soul. Our marriage ended before our second anniversary, but it took years to recover from the emotional damage.

When I finally began to focus on me, though, on healing and moving on rather than saving an unsavable marriage, my whole body relaxed. I occupied more of the space around me, feeling comfortable and open. I leaned into conversations or sat back and used the armrests. I was unselfconscious. My voice softened because I'd surrendered my defensiveness.

In the early days of our work together, my therapist worked hard to help me regain my sense of self. He was the person to introduce me to the concept of mindfulness and intentional living. He taught me that I could change my future by simply choosing to be present now. There was no mystery or magic cure. I didn't need to do anything other than show up for myself and participate. I learned that moving through the days with mindfulness and intention were the keys to my power. To living life in a way that would eventually bring peace.

It was during my work with him that I discovered how emotional trauma impacts the physical body. For years, I suffered from migraines, digestive issues, disordered sleeping, hair loss, and a host of other problems that led to countless doctor's visits and, almost always, yet another prescription. Beyond the stresses that trauma puts on the body, routinely swallowing my emotions and trying to power through on my own had left me trapped in a cycle of both mental and physical pain and suffering. Breaking free required patience, diligence, and constant work.

Healer

Six months after my impulsive visit to the Priestess in New Orleans, and just a few days before Christmas, I saw a woman who worked as an intuitive energy healer. A friend told me about her and made appointments for us both under one name. The first time the healer heard mine was when I introduced myself as I was being led back. She worked out of a massage treatment room in a salon and spa business. The space was softly lit with candles and a strand of clear holiday lights strung against a dark ceiling. The air was scented with essential oils.

I sat in the chair across from hers, armed with a notebook and pen and ready to document everything she said. She walked me through her process and how she prepares to meet with clients. She talked of allowing herself to tune in and connect with the universe and her client's energy. As part of her mental prep, she receives music or a song specific to each person and where they are in their journey.

Over the next two hours I took eight pages of notes as she told me things about myself and my world that I had never shared with a soul. She described me as contracted with the universe to be a "sensitive" mixed with "spirit and fire", meaning I'm a passionate empath. She also said that her first sense was that I am an abuse survivor, going on to describe the emotional processing survivors go through as mourning a death.

"It's time to let that go," she said. "Pay your respects to what you've been through, then free yourself to embrace peace, joy, adventure, and travel. Spend time learning about yourself to find what brings you authentic joy. Focus on manifesting that instead of continuing to search your past for clues and fresh sources of pain."

I continued note-taking, trying to capture every word, and nodding as she spoke.

"You need to purge your house of negativity," she said. "There's something in your bathroom that's bringing negative energy connected to your past. Get rid of it. It's got to go."

I was instantly offended and a little hurt. "I just had my bathroom totally redone," I said. "I love it."

She was unfazed by my defensiveness. "There's something negative in there. I don't know what, but there's something in it that needs to go." I was mentally picturing everything in my bathroom. None of it came from the ex, and by the time I'd had it redone we weren't even speaking. She moved on to things that ran the gamut from cookie cutter generalities to disarmingly accurate insights. I continued taking copious notes, and then it hit me.

"Oh, my God. The shower curtain and hooks," I interrupted. "I had them when I was married. I kept them because I liked the color, and they went with the remodel."

"They have to go," she said. "You see them every day. It's not good to start your day looking at a reminder of your old life."

Her face grew serious as she continued to talk about my ex. She spoke of how dark his energy is and how crucial it is for my survival to have gotten away from him. "He's got the darkest energy I've ever seen," she said, describing images of a stabbing violence to my heart that came to her when I talked about him. She said my energy reminded her of a burn victim who was scarred everywhere. The analogy surprised me, but I didn't say anything. What she could not have known was that my ex set fire to some of my things when I finally left him for good. He recorded it, and then sent me the video so that I could watch it all burn. It was my punishment for leaving, and the first in a series of rages over the next year that were part of his scorched earth approach to our split.

Near the end of my appointment, the healer had me get on the massage table for energy work. It involved repeating a series of affirmations intended to release the final bits of negativity and replacing them with hope. When she was done, she reached for her phone to play the song that came to her when she was preparing for my session. She asked me to listen, let the tears flow if they came, and to take my time. She reminded me that her work is intended to stir up deep feelings and heal wounds, so it would be natural to feel a bit emotionally drained after.

She dimmed the lights further and left the room. I heard Rihanna's voice singing the first lines to "Love the Way You Lie" and cried deep, body-shaking tears.

When I left, I was an emotionally exhausted mess. I met my friend for a quick recap of our respective sessions, but really needed to be alone to process. I drove straight to Bed, Bath, and Beyond to get a new shower curtain, downloading the song on the way. I played it over and over again, eventually coming to know the lyrics by heart. For weeks after, I listened to that song nonstop and let myself feel. Sometimes I tried to sing along but could never get past the first few lines without crying. Even now, every time I hear it, I am transported right back to the me who lost so much of herself trying to be loved by people incapable of offering anything but pain.

Courage

In the spring of 2018, I left for two weeks in Luxembourg, Belgium, and the Netherlands—a trip where I would find the courage to change my life. I felt the familiar invigorating rush of being alive again when I landed in Amsterdam. It was time for a new adventure, but I was also anxious to get to the root of some heavy feelings shadowing what seemed to be an otherwise happy time in my life. Although I booked a tour for most of the trip, I had decided to explore tiny Luxembourg and beautiful Brussels on my own.

I spent the first few days in my usual travel cycle of tired, lost, overwhelmed, excited, inspired, and finally exhilarated. Luxembourg City was glorious. I'm determined to go back one day to explore it properly. My adventure there was cut short when I got on the right bus headed the wrong way because I can't read or speak French or Luxembourgish. I did get the opportunity to play charades with the bus driver while trying to communicate that I needed to go to the train station, not the suburbs. It cost me a couple hours of precious sightseeing time before catching my train to Brussels, but it's a great memory.

Once I finally made it to Brussels, having figured out which of the three train stations in the city was closest to my hotel, I had a tiny freak out moment over logistics. My map app was trying to give me directions to walk the mile from the train station but none of the streets appeared to be named. It didn't help that whoever designed medieval cities in Europe seemed to have a had a bias against square city blocks or long streets. Any instruction was only accurate for a handful of steps. I got lost, turned around, and lost again.

One of my most vivid memories is standing in the middle of downtown Brussels, exhausted and dragging my suitcase over cobblestones, stopping every few steps to look at my phone, then alternating between staring at it and looking around desperately for clues, or help. *I'm a smart woman*, I remember telling myself as I started to feel overwhelmed by jetlag, frustration, and just a little bit of panic, *I can figure this out.* In the end, it took over an hour to find the place my map app kept insisting was only twenty minutes away. But I found it, and that's what matters. After I checked in, I celebrated my navigational victory with an amazing glass of red wine in the hotel bar.

One of the many things I have come to love about traveling alone is that it requires me to push past my anxiety and self-doubt. Solo travel insists that I step up and conquer, and that challenge invigorates me. It pushes me to be better, because having only myself to rely on means acknowledging that I am also the only person standing in my way. It requires me to have faith in my abilities, especially in areas where I would normally rely on someone else.

When I was first exploring Brussels, my familiar feelings of anxiety and insecurity started to surface, but I chose to be kind to myself. When I got lost trying to find the Grand Market Place at city center, I took a deep breath and allowed myself a moment's pause. I did the same when I felt overwhelmed by the crowds. No one was with me to get mad at unexpected detours or blame me for ruining the day. Nothing life-altering happened when I turned down a wrong street or chose a meal that was less than perfect. The world didn't end. The sky didn't fall. Instead, choosing to see everything as part of the adventure, as a surprise waiting to unfold, made every encounter even better. And, though I was lonely at times, Brussels was beautiful, and everyone was kind and helpful, as much as the language barrier would allow.

I spent two days in Brussels then took the train to Ghent to meet up with my tour group. The city itself is magical and medieval, with hints of modern thrown in for added shine. I left my bags at the hotel then went straight to Sint Veerleplein Square to have lunch and a glass of wine in front of Gravensteen Castle. Since I'd done no research on Ghent, I had no idea there was a medieval castle in the middle of town until seeing it from the backseat of the cab. I didn't know I was stepping into history and spending a few days in a beautiful, balanced fusion of old and new. It was a glorious surprise. When I got to the square, I sat at an outdoor table to look around and marvel.

The castle was perfect, like something out of a storybook. It's a citadel fortress made of stone, complete with turrets and arrow slits, and designed to be imposing. Meant to intimidate and allow for defense against all manner of attack. It even has a moat that's fed from the Lys river, providing an extra source of protection from unknown invaders many hundreds of years ago. I allowed myself to imagine the world as it was then, archers perched atop the turrets, ready to shoot their arrows into anyone who came too close. The iron chains rattling with the raising of the drawbridge, securing the safety of those inside.

While it may have been designed for battle, this place they call the Castle of the Counts reminded me a bit of Cinderella's castle. I found it romantic, set as it was against the glow from the sunshine of a warm spring afternoon. I lingered in the public square in front of its grounds until dusk when the castle's lights came up, brightening it against the evening sky. The illumination made it look enchanted, and I felt like I was vacationing in the middle of a fairytale.

It was in the breakfast room of our very modern hotel where I first met Jane and her husband the next morning. They were part of the tour group and introduced themselves right away. After our guide led us on a city tour the ended at the Museum of Fine Arts, Jane and I found ourselves sharing stories about life in the real world during the walk back. I mentioned my corporate career and how unfulfilled I was feeling day-to-day. I was unhappy at work and feeling empty and increasingly disconnected in the rest of my life. I was also finding that with my children grown and into their own lives, the only person left to take care of was me. I was genuinely lost on how to do that. I knew how to be a mom, friend, or provider. I knew how to take care of other people but didn't know how to prioritize taking care of me. I was at a crossroads. A place where self-care as a matter of survival was starting to look different from taking care of and nurturing myself as a matter of truly living.

Jane casually commented that I sounded "so done." Her straightforward observation hit hard. She'd named the feeling I hoped to get to the bottom of while on this trip, that shadow that had been clouding my world. I knew the only thing standing in the way of living the life I wanted was the fear of letting go of the life I had always known. So, the next day, with twenty seconds of the insane bravery that only comes with knowing there is no going back, I called my boss to quit my job. She listened, then very politely declined to accept my resignation, and told me to enjoy the rest of my vacation. I spent the next two weeks exploring Belgium and the Netherlands with the tour group. Happily dividing my time between the excitement of my European adventures and planning for the ones that would start once I returned home.

I resigned a second time within hours of starting my first day back to work. Despite the many, many, *many* stumbles that followed, it is a decision I have never once regretted. Travel has brought me back to life. It has given me life. It has reminded me who I am. It has provided a timely, divine resurrection every time I have needed one.

Faith

I was raised in a churchgoing family. As kids, we faithfully attended Sunday School, regular church services, Vacation Bible School, and most midweek youth activities. It was a primary part of our social life. We were baptized Lutheran, but our family was also part of the congregation at our local community church. Growing up, I attended nondenominational church services as well as those in several of the faiths under the umbrella of Christianity. I considered us more general churchgoers than devout to any specific denomination. By thirteen, I was taking classes for confirmation in the Lutheran faith, which would make me an adult in the eyes of the church. I was excited because it focused on the history of Lutheranism, which I found fascinating. But the best thing about being confirmed was that I could stop going to church, because adults get to make their own decisions.

I had grown disillusioned with religion at an early age. I watched people who did not live their faith preach the loudest on Sundays. I saw sanctimony partner with an eagerness to judge and condemn those who did not go to church, or who were not Christian. I listened week after week as conversation during the after-service coffee hour was more gossip than gospel. It all seemed to be less about faith than about power, judgement, control, and exclusion. Things that were contrary to what I was being taught about Christ and Christianity.

Perhaps the most important thing I discovered during confirmation was that if the concepts of traditional church and religion were not for me, maybe faith was, and maybe faith was something very different than what I was seeing played out in my community. I didn't explore it much at the time because all I really wanted to do was stop going to church, and it was decades before I revisited the idea of faith as something separate from a Sunday service.

Today, I consider myself spiritually agnostic more than anything else. Hellfire and brimstone, and those who preach it, have no place in my world. Dogma and rhetoric won't hold my interest. Authenticity and genuine devotion will. While I no longer attend church services, I never miss an opportunity to visit places of worship when I travel, especially cathedrals. I'm drawn to the buildings and always find a quiet, comforting peace within their walls that I have never felt in a modern church. I allow myself to walk through them silently, even reverently, absorbing their history and beauty.

What I experience as faith comes in the calm, quiet moments when I'm on the edge of change. It comes from trusting signs and listening to the messages from people who have been put in my path to deliver. It comes from choosing to surrender and accept peace. It comes from the knowledge that I already have everything I need to live the life I want. For me, faith is in the everyday—not in a sermon or a building.

Despite all my years of traveling and visiting every religious structure I could along the way, I have never been one to light candles. A visit to St. James' Church in Bruges changed that. It was a few days after my breakthrough talk with Jane. I was feeling peaceful and exhilarated while I explored the town on my own. I had come to the decision to change my life, and I could rest in both ease and excitement knowing my way forward. I had no real plan for the day other than to wander around and see what I saw when I turned a corner and there it was, almost hidden, nestled quietly at the end of the street. It's Gothic by design, with a beautiful stone exterior that blends seamlessly into the surrounding architecture. It's simple and elegant, not attention grabbing or imposing. I was drawn in by its peaceful humility, entering through the red front doors.

Inside, the church was filled with masterpieces of intricate woodwork, period paintings, triptychs, and soaring ceilings. It was cool and mostly empty inside, providing a bit of respite from fellow travelers and from an unseasonably hot May afternoon. I took my time looking around, marveling as I had done in countless other churches over the years, then walked toward the door.

I had taken just a few steps outside when I felt an overwhelming need to turn around and go back in. I walked toward the altar and sat at the end of a hard pew, thinking about nothing and everything at the same time. My mind had started racing with all the familiar negative, toxic thoughts that had appeared after deciding to confidently, if impulsively, change my life. I knew I'd done what I had to, but I didn't know what was going to happen next or where to even start. I was scared. I was relieved. But mostly I was exhausted from having tried so hard to white knuckle my way to happiness.

In a moment of surrender, I closed my eyes and allowed my mind to clear. I focused on the future. On channeling hope. On believing I deserve good things, and on trusting they will happen. When I was done, I slipped a one-euro coin in the box and lit a candle. For myself.

Call it prayer. Call it meditation. Call it any word that fits. What I call it is the first time I chose to let go and surrender to something bigger than me. The first time I chose to have faith.

Snow Globes

That New Year's Eve, I met with the healer again. Life was dramatically different than it had been during my first visit twelve months earlier, but I felt more lost than ever. After Belgium, I'd followed through and quit my job. I dove headfirst into a dream I hadn't known I had and opened a wellness center. A place wholly devoted to self-care. I thought leaving my job would bring me peace since it had been so toxic in recent years. I thought doing something for me and no one else would make me happy. It didn't.

I was miserable and stressed all the time. I may have hated my old job, but at least it came with a steady check. Now, I was chasing a dream and working for myself but not making a cent. My physical health was suffering. Mentally, I was a mess and beginning to have deep doubts about myself and my ability to succeed. I tried every day to be strong and stay positive because I had always been able to power through. Survivorship was the hallmark of my life. I'd been successful in school and my career, some-times through the force of sheer willpower alone. But launching a business was terrifying, and I was failing. Every insecurity of the last forty years was bubbling up and threatening to take over. 2018 had kicked my ass and I needed a reset if I wanted to start 2019 in hope.

So once again, I sat in the healer's room asking for sup-port and insight. Anything to help me understand why it all continued to be so damned hard. She was patient and kind, telling me calmly that I'd met my transformation at warp speed and the rest of me was still trying to catch up. She reminded me of the power of free will then took me through a visualization exercise. In choosing to change my life all at once, I shook the snow globe that is my universe. The chaos, pain, and panic were the snowflakes floating about, freshly shaken and clouding my view but slowly settling into place. All I needed to do was be patient, keep my eyes forward, and have faith.

The second part of our session focused on my mom. At the time, I was three years removed from that New Year's Eve breakfast, but no closer to peace or my father's name. I hadn't allowed myself to acknowledge how much I was truly suffering. But, when I forced myself to accept that she was more worried about who I'd told than she was about how it affected me, my heart broke.

My healer focused in on that energy. She saw an origin story vastly different from the rape one I had been giv-en. What she saw was an affair while both were married to other people, and a surprise pregnancy he never knew about. They ran in the same circles and knew many of the same people. He was older than Mom and my healer was certain he was still alive, so she was also certain we would one day meet. She sensed my mom's emotional detach-ment toward me was because I'm a daily reminder of lost possibilities. She resents what I represent but loves me as much as she is able. Our session closed with affirmations and energy work, along with a bit of a warning: pushing Mom further will likely end our relationship. She is not emotionally capable of giving me what I need.

I knew as she spoke every word was true. I am here because of a forbidden affair, not because of sexual violence. I knew it because the soul always recognizes truth.

Six months later, when my DNA dad and I had our first phone conversation, he told me the story of their relationship, and unknowingly confirmed nearly everything my healer said.

Disneyland

Four months later, in the spring of 2019, Mom celebrated turning 70 in Disneyland with all of her kids and grandkids. I was thrilled to spend time with my boys, and I suppose the rest of the family enjoyed the trip, but my resentment toward her was bubbling into a rage. It was hard to be kind to her. I couldn't look her in the eyes and I'd long outgrown being patient with her. So, I played along for the pictures and a few group activities but kept my distance.

My life was a mess. I was about to close my business, and I was panicked over how I'd recover. But that was secondary to how much I was struggling with my identity. I was freshly consumed with a need to know the truth. I needed to know more, even if I never met the man who fathered me. I wanted her to tell me what happened. I wanted her to answer my questions. To give me comfort and help me understand. What fueled my resentment was knowing she never would. I knew she was lying. Her story had evolved so many times in the years since that New Year's Eve breakfast that her lies just became more and more obvious. The fact that she would rather lie than tell the truth, especially when she knew how much it was hurting me, made me hate her. Which made me feel awful about myself.

I decided Disneyland was a line in the sand. I would give her the birthday celebration she wanted. I'd participate in the family photos that she was sure to post all over social media and send out as Christmas cards. But after that, we were having a conversation. I was done with her being a roadblock. She needed to know that with or without her help, I planned to find out the truth. That meant doing whatever it took, including talking about what I knew with people who knew her then.

I called her the day after I got home. She was with my stepdad in the airport waiting to catch her flight.

"What's going on?" She asked. "Is everything okay?"

"I didn't know you weren't home yet. I wanted to wait until after the trip to talk to you," I said, trying to sound calm and cool. Matter of fact, even. "I need to let you know that I'm going to try to find my dad."

"Honey, I told you. I don't know who he is."

Her voice sounded like it did when I was a little girl. When she was trying to project maternal warmth and comfort. It almost soothed me into backing down because even after all I've been through, I still hate upsetting people.

"I can't keep feeling like this, Mom." I said, tears welling up. "I need to know."

I got off my couch and started pacing my living room the way I always do when a conversation has me emotional.

"I can't tell you what I don't know, honey. I'm sorry. I know you're upset with me. I can feel it."

"Because I know you know more than you're telling me!" I cried. "And I don't understand why you won't help me!"

I started to hyperventilate. I was crying so hard I couldn't speak. "Please Mom! Tell me something!" I begged. "I need to know who I am!"

I was sobbing uncontrollably. I needed my mommy. I needed her to care that I was broken and begging. I was pleading with her to love me enough to tell me the truth. I couldn't catch my breath. I couldn't stop the tears. I couldn't stop the agony. But she said nothing while I laid myself bare. She stayed silent while my heart broke, leaving me with only the sounds of background flight announcements as a response.

"Mom, please." I begged in a shattered voice when I was finally calm enough to find words.

"Okay honey. Let me talk to some of the women I used to work with. I think they knew him."

What?

"Wait. You still talk to them? Why didn't you call them four years ago? I don't understand." My broken tears were waning, replaced by a flood of fresh frustration and disbelief.

"I didn't think about it at the time. But let me call them and see what they remember."

"I'm confused. You said you only saw him that one time."

"I did. But they knew who he was."

"Okay. Please call them" I said. "But I need you to know that I'm not stopping until I find out."

"Honey, please just wait and let me talk to them first. Let's see what they know and go from there." She said, like she was suddenly my ally. "They're calling our flight. I have to go. I love you."

"Love you, too, Mom."

I dropped my phone on the coffee table and collapsed back onto the couch, exhausted. A few minutes later, I got a text alert. It was Mom.

"We are on the plane. Are you ok?"

I stared at it in disbelief. What was wrong with her? How could she even ask a question like that after the conversation we just had? I started to type out a whole response detailing exactly how I was feeling and why. Flight departure be damned, I still had things to say. Then I realized I'd already given her too much.

She let her child hyperventilate. She let her child beg. She let her child cry in absolute agony. And she did it all knowing she was the one who could provide peace and relief. She chose her lies over comforting her child. I'm a mom and I'd sooner die than be the reason my kids are in pain. That conversation broke something in me. I knew I'd never forgive her.

I deleted everything I'd written, typed "no", and touched the blue arrow to send.

Mystery DNA

I don't know what I thought I would find when I finally discovered who fathered me. I didn't even know how I would find him. It was clear early on that Mom would be of no help. She was working very hard to keep her stories straight, so there was no chance she would voluntarily share anything.

As is the way with life, the truth came rather unexpectedly. A few weeks after Disneyland, and the heartbreaking call with Mom that followed, I did Ancestry.com for a second time. I did 23&Me, too, because I knew Mom had done it and thought I might have better luck there. I quickly found third and fourth cousins on 23&Me but had a hard time figuring out if they were on Mom's side since she had deleted all her own information. Some early leads that seemed promising turned out to be dead ends, which was both frustrating and exactly what I expected.

My Ancestry.com results were a different story. To my surprise, Erica had left her profile active from four years earlier, which meant I had a screening tool for future hits. As soon as my new results posted, I was notified of a match for a possible half-sibling. A new sister. I quickly checked Erica's tree to see if this person matched to her as well.

Nope.

New Sister was connected to me through my Mystery DNA. I reached out through the site's messaging platform immediately, sending a generic message no different than the countless ones I'd received from new matches hoping to explore how we were related. No response. I sent another message a few weeks later, but again, nothing.

I cannot begin to count the number of times I stared at New Sister's screen name and locked profile thinking this was the end. I met Steven, one of my brothers, for drinks and talked about accepting that a screen name was as close as I would ever get to answers. Oddly enough, I had made peace with the idea and was fine with never knowing more. The journey was about me and uncovering who I am, not finding a new family. Discovering New Sister then not seeing her on Erica's tree validated a truth I'd known in my soul. It freed me in ways that are nearly impossible to describe other than to say it gave me validation. I was right. No amount of gaslighting by my mother would undo that fact.

Days after seeing Steven, I received a message from a woman working on a family tree. She was hoping to figure out how I was related to her daughter. After some investigative messaging back and forth, we determined that it was through my paternal side. I said I couldn't help more since I was on the site to find my dad and had hit a dead end of my own. I told her about the screen name, the locked profile, and the unreturned messages then apologized for not being able to do more. She replied within minutes, saying, "I recognize that screen name. I think I know who that is. Her dad's name is Carl..."

With those few sentences, and after years of searching, a stranger on the internet gave me what my own mother would not. I stared at the screen waiting for the emotion to come.

Any emotion. Anything at all.

I felt nothing. Once again, I had automatically gone on autopilot and turned into a robot. I eventually remembered my manners, emailing back to thank her for giving me the last piece to a six-year long puzzle. She was sympathetic and gracious when she replied, filling in a few blanks like what area he lived in and what he'd done for work. She also told me she had never met him. Apparently, there was a rift between him and the side of the family she married into that went back decades. The message closed with his mailing address and this: "he's been married for over fifty years, so be prepared for some hostility."

I texted Mom, angry and determined to call her out.

"I found my dad. His name is Carl. He's from around here. You and Gene knew him, which explains why all you cared about that day was me not telling anyone and deleting my profile. You didn't give a shit about the pain your daughter has been in. All you cared about is covering your ass and protecting your lie."

She never responded.

I sent a lot of texts over the next few days. Not because I was afraid to call her, but because the only way to be heard in a difficult conversation with her was to write. The last thing I needed was to hear more lies and excuses. I didn't need to be shut down before I had a chance to speak. I wanted her to hear me. I needed her to feel and understand my pain. And, yes, in the back of my mind I still hoped she would finally own up to almost fifty years of lies.

She didn't. In fact, nothing I said made an impact. She alternated between evolving her lies to fit the current fact pattern and outright ignoring me. It was another reminder that my mother does not do personal accountability. Ever.

A New Life & DNA Dad

I moved to Seattle about two weeks before learning my DNA Dad's name, and six months after my last visit to the healer. Life had been in full upheaval for a year by that point, ever since leaving the stability and security of my corporate job to open my own business. My soul forced me to see the need to keep living life in the present, but it did not prepare me for what I was about to go through.

My business didn't succeed in its initial stage for all the reasons all the experts say. It was a startup with an untested concept, not enough cash flow, and too much overhead. When I closed the door on that chapter of my dream, I was faced with a life I didn't recognize. My kids were grown and into lives of their own. My finances were fully upside down for the first time since I'd rebuilt my life after my second divorce. This time, though, I no longer had the corporate job, with the corporate paycheck and corporate benefits, to rely on while I put it all back together. I had no idea who I was or what to do next. I was on the verge of losing everything, and all because I wanted to find myself and start a new life.

For weeks after I closed the doors, I sat on my couch, knees curled to my chest, in a panicked but frozen stupor. I started sleeping twelve and fourteen hours at a stretch. My big move of the day was getting out of bed to take up residence in the living room. I forced myself to get out and walk for at least an hour most days, which became my justification for having just one more drink at night.

Friends and family were steadfast in reaching out to offer love and support. Thanks to their generosity, I took a couple of weekend trips meant to see if I could plug back into life again. During dinners or walks or even deep conversations, I faked my way through with forced smiles and promises that everything will be fine. Really. It's nothing more than a phase. No need to worry. In truth, I was an absolute zombie, barely going through the motions of living.

"Here we go again," I thought as I updated my resume and started applying to every job in town. I had no desire to work in my old field again. It wasn't bad work. It just wasn't fulfilling anymore. But what choice did I have? I'd taken a risk and failed, so now I was buried under a mountain of debt with no more savings and the only way to get back on my feet was to go back to the corporate paycheck. I spent hours each day looking for work. All the while, my negativity was on overdrive. Repeating the same tired toxic messages on a nonstop loop. *What was I thinking? People like me don't succeed. That's saved for other people.* I said it to myself so many times that I came to believe it as much or more than I ever had before.

Eventually one of my friends asked an obvious question, but one that hadn't occurred to me in my misery. "Do you think you're done with this place? Is it time to move?" She was right. I was done. Her question, asked with nothing but my peace and happiness at heart, was permission to think beyond the twenty-five-mile radius where I'd focused my job search. It allowed me to see moving as starting anew versus running away. I broadened my search after that, applying to everything I was qualified for from Hawaii to Puerto Rico. I decided I was going to let the universe tell me where I belonged instead of trying to force fit something that would once again make me miserable.

A few weeks later, I accepted a job in Seattle. I had reservations and a knot in my stomach the day of the onsite interview but told myself it was nothing more than nerves that needed to be overcome. So once again, I took a risk and went for it.

By the time I discovered DNA Dad, I had gone from living in a 2000 square foot house on a corner lot across the street from a quiet and well-kept city park, to a 488 square foot studio apartment in a mixed-use building above a Total Wine store.

I could feel my life changing as soon as I decided to move. Every day was something new. But transformation is notoriously unsteady, and I had no idea where it would take me or who I'd be at the end. I started my new job, but knew it was a bad fit within the first five minutes of day one. It didn't matter. I committed myself to doing whatever it took to make it work because taking that job got me to Seattle and I felt certain I was supposed to be here.

Outside of trying to figure out how to quiet the noise my intuition was making about my job, I spent time each day creating a new routine for my new life. One that didn't cost much, as total financial ruin was still one missed paycheck away. I went on walks to explore the neighborhood and found a grocery store I liked. I searched for a hairstylist who understood how to cut curly hair. I tried out yoga studios where I was freshly reminded that hot yoga and I do not mix, and I made friends with a couple of amazing women at work. And when I was home alone at night, trying to quiet the noise, I reminded myself that a new life in Seattle had to work because I was out of options.

One night, in the middle of all of this, I wrote a letter to my DNA Dad. I introduced myself and stated my case. I was clear that I wanted nothing. Not a relationship. Not money. Nothing. My lone intent was to have my existence be known. For once in my life, I was demanding to be seen. I included a picture of me, smiling and happy, and mailed it with no return address the next day. I started to feel some peace after that, and even some pride in having finally solved the puzzle. My quest was never about finding daddy and getting a childhood redo. It was about the truth and unravelling the lie that had formed the foundation of my soul.

The days after mailing the letter brought fresh determination and an overwhelming sense of calm. I had my answers now. Everything about my life suddenly made much more sense. I spent hours looking back on experiences through a different lens. I discarded the one that framed everything as me being broken, and instead reveled in the clarity of the truth. I knew why I had a lifelong struggle with trust. I knew why I was drawn to narcissists, and why their uncertainty and chaos felt like home. I understood why I felt like I had to earn love and why I was always scared it would be taken away. And I finally knew why I trusted the comfort of strangers more than the love of my mother.

I wasn't crazy. I wasn't damaged or broken or bad. I was raised in a lie and somewhere in my soul, I had always known it even if I didn't know what it meant. I felt like a bird freed from a cage.

My new mission was to create a life that felt true. A life that wouldn't require me to sacrifice anything about who I am. I made a promise to myself that I would trust my intuition without question from now on because ignoring it had meant choosing pain. Every single time.

Right around this time, I started receiving calls from a number I didn't recognize in a town where I knew no one. I don't answer calls from numbers that aren't already in my phone unless I'm job hunting, so I sent it to voicemail. This went on for a little over a week with the calls coming at roughly the same time each day. I eventually blocked the number thinking it was an oddly persistent robo-caller and didn't give it another thought.

A few days after that, I was at work clearing out deleted voicemails while on a break and saw I had a new folder in my mailbox titled "blocked voicemails". Turns out my robo-caller left three messages. I decided to listen to the most recent one to find out what they were selling before deleting them all.

"Hello," the voice began, "this is Carl, but you can call me Dad. I hear you've been looking for me..."

Holy shit.

I listened to the message a second time. He was going to be out of cell service for a few days but would call later. He said he had a favor to ask of me.

How the hell did he get my phone number?

He didn't call that night. The message was three days old by the time I listened to it, so I assumed he changed his mind about talking. Calling him never crossed mine. I wasn't sure I even wanted to talk to him. Somewhere deep in my soul, I felt something telling me not to pull at that thread.

He called the next night. The first thing he asked me to do was lie about my age if I ever talked to his wife. Somehow, me being a year older would make my existence more palatable to the woman he'd been with longer than I'd been alive. That was the favor he was referring to in his voicemail. I said I wouldn't lie and couldn't be sure she'd never find out, but I wouldn't be the one to tell her. That seemed to appease him. We talked for almost two hours. He told me how he met my mom and the circumstances of their relationship. He validated the core assumption I'd made years ago, and what my healer said was true. I was the product of an affair, not a rape. They ran in the same circles and their spouses knew each other. He swore he knew nothing about me, but I am wanted and loved. He had my number because Mom gave it to him.

We talked and texted over the next few days. I shared the highlights of my life and he told me more details about him and Mom. That quiet but insistent warning from my soul surfaced again. It wasn't screaming, so I ignored it. I learned Mom sent him family Christmas pictures for at least a few years after I was born. She also called him when I was nine to ask about his blood type because, in her words, "my daughter's sick and she's got a rare one". He said his response was, "what the fuck does that have to do with me?"

We had a few conversations over the next several days that undermined his story of knowing nothing about me, but he stood by it and I didn't push because I didn't care. I was tired of forcing people to acknowledge me, so listening to someone else rationalize away my existence didn't hold my interest. He and Mom could make peace with the lies they had told everyone, including themselves. I wasn't taking it on.

After the first handful of conversations, I started paying attention to my inner voice. It was trying to get me to see something, but I wasn't sure what. I started noticing that while he said he was so excited to have a daughter, he never asked questions about me. We talked about him. About the upheaval in his life since finding out about me. About how his wife took the news. About how she reacted days later when he had to come clean about my age after having his hand forced by his oldest daughter—the half-sister behind the locked screen name on Ancestry. com. We talked about how his daughters took the news. We talked about his childhood, his marital problems, and everything else about his life. We did not talk about me.

Even if he asked a question, we would be talking about him again within minutes. I chalked it all up to loneliness and nerves. He was almost eighty, after all. I just figured he needed someone to talk to since he said he had no meaningful relationship with his other kids. He also said he couldn't talk to his wife because she was having a hard time with it all.

So, I shifted gears and went into listener mode because this connection was no longer about me finding my dad. I felt my walls go up and my autopilot come on like a protective forcefield. Despite how excited he claimed to be about having a new daughter and how much he said he loved me, he was focused only on him. Our conversations settled into a pattern where he would ask a question or two, then talk about his marriage and himself.

He wanted to meet. We lived on opposite sides of the state, so the logistics took a bit. Plans got canceled once because his wife wasn't ready. They were almost canceled a second time because she insisted on coming with. Once again, I felt myself swallow my needs to accommodate someone else's feelings. Here I was making plans to meet my father for the first time, and how I felt was less important than his wife insisting on being included.

My inner voice was getting louder. I continued to ignore it because despite years of doing the work, diminishing my own needs to be accepted by others was still my default.

A month later, we met in a grocery store parking lot roughly halfway between his side of the state and mine. It was anticlimactic. I was back on autopilot and fully indifferent. He was so excited to see me, but I felt numb. I put on the same face I used when I worked in customer service – frozen smile and forced interest. By then, I knew how much he just wanted someone to talk with, so I asked questions and kept the conversation moving.

My autopilot started to falter after a couple of hours. It left me with a sudden, urgent desire to get away. I felt overwhelmed and under so much pressure to be someone I wasn't to please this man who wanted his new daughter so badly. He was talking to me and holding my hands like we had a lifelong connection while all I saw when I looked at him was a stranger. A kind old man, but a stranger.

He was visibly upset and a little angry when I brought our visit to a close. It seems he and his wife had envisioned us having a first meeting that carried on into the late hours of the night. It was barely noon and I was out of things to say. I drove home feeling like I had completed an errand.

PART IV: LIGHT

Maybe you have to know the darkness before you can appreciate the light.
— Madeline L'Engle

One Hundred Days

One of the ways I keep going when life is dark is to remind myself that everything passes eventually. I know now that pain doesn't last forever, despite how it feels when in the thick of it. Neither does happiness. The only way to appreciate the light is to learn from the dark. During one of my worst days after moving to Seattle, I put a note in my calendar marking one hundred days out. Not because I believed life would magically be better on day one hundred. I knew it wasn't that simple. But because I needed to hang on to something to remind myself that there was life after pain. That good would come again.

I pushed myself to reflect on what I had already overcome, journaling obsessively to purge the darkest of my thoughts. I relied on my friends to listen, love, and support. I let myself pull away and shut down when I needed to care for myself. For the first time in my life, I gave myself permission to feel exactly what I felt in the moment I felt it. I did it without apology or explanation, finally not caring what anyone thought. I told myself I had done my part. I'd honored every commitment I'd ever made, so now that my kids were in their own lives, I could focus solely on me. But how? Having never done that on full time basis before, I was terrified.

I was unemployed at the time, so healing and choosing a new future became my job. I hated it at first. It didn't pay, the hours were insane, and I was required to work from home all day, every day. The boss was kind of an asshole, too. But a lifetime of lies had unraveled in tandem with a full eighteen months of professional and personal upheaval, all of which were now demanding my focus. I'd blown up my life. It seemed only right that I take the time to process and put it back together the right way.

Ultimately, the darkness of those days was one of the great blessings of my life. I see it now as the universe's way of making sure I stayed focused and did the work. I remember the moment a few weeks in when I started to feel genuine hope versus going through the motions on autopilot, still trying to endure. It was the end of October. The leaves were changing, the fall air was crisp. I was on my daily walk by the lake and felt a rush of peace take over. Suddenly, I wasn't numb or scared anymore. I wasn't in pain and I wasn't sad. I was certain, finally, that I would be okay. In that moment, I wasn't worried anymore.

From the outside, nothing had changed. I still had no answers. I wasn't sure how the bills were going to be paid or what was going happen next, but I had no doubt it would all be fine. I took a few pictures of the leaves and posted them to Instagram with the caption "my favorite season" then went home a hundred pounds lighter and filled with hope.

On day one hundred, I started the job that would allow me to recover financially.

The Bottom Below Rock Bottom

The Monday after I met Carl, I gave notice at my job.
The job that got me to Seattle. The one I knew immediately was a bad fit. That one. That job. I'd had it two
months. When it came to my career, I had never been
reckless or impulsive. Had I done reckless and impulsive things in the rest of my life? Yes, absolutely. But
my career? The thing that allowed me to provide for my
children and was one of my few sources of confidence?
Never.

Yet there I was, telling the man who recruited me
only months earlier that I was leaving. The job was not
the right fit for me, I told him. I gave him an explanation that included most of the reasons why. What I left
out, what I lacked the courage to say even when asked
directly, was that I was leaving in part because of him.

When I left the corporate world after my return from Belgium, it was because my intuition was demanding that I stop settling. I had begun to feel unvalued and was treated poorly at work. Which was doubly painful since my personal life was a mess and at a lonely crossroads of its own. Choosing to walk away to follow a dream was liberating. It was also terrifying. In the year that passed between that job and this one, I changed. I was past the point in my life where I would accept poor treatment in exchange for a paycheck. I promised myself that I would never again swallow toxicity to keep the peace. I had worth. I had value. I deserved respect and a seat at the table. I knew I had to go back to the corporate world to recover financially and start over, but swore I wouldn't settle, because all my dues were paid.

Yet when push came to shove, I accepted a role that my gut said was wrong because it was going to get me where I needed to go. I rationalized away the noise and told myself I'd do it for a year and then find something else. Once again, I compromised. I accepted less because I was scared. I didn't trust that another opportunity would come my way. I didn't trust my worth.

I was miserable there from the beginning. Culturally, it was not the place for me. Even so, I did my best to get through the days by reminding myself it was one year. I could do anything for a year. Betraying myself again was as easy as that. In the span of a few seemingly small choices, I silenced myself, and the cycle began all over again. Little by little, day by day, I went to work and compromised a bit more of who I am just to keep the peace. The fear of losing my job made me sacrifice my voice. I made myself small and obedient.

I said nothing in meetings that were antagonistic, bordering on harassing, because I was new and needed to learn. I said nothing when the passive-aggressive comments started. I accepted the hot and cold personality of my boss because it was nothing unusual for me. I hated it, but I was used to it. I said nothing when the snarky commentary began about what I had or had not done in my past work experience. Even when the snarky commentator was wrong, I said nothing. I said nothing when the misogyny of the entitled, religious middle-aged male executives became pervasive and too blatant to ignore. From daily casual innuendo to comments about why women shouldn't be allowed to do certain things. From 'accidentally' grazing the side of my breast during a walk to saying, "do you work out?" while staring with a tilted head at my ass. Through it all, I said nothing. Until my inner voice started screaming and forced me to do something.

Still, when the chief executive officer/breast grazer asked if I was leaving because of him or something he had done, I said no. I laid it mostly at the feet of the snarky commentator rather than share the bigger truth that I was leaving because the culture was a nightmare. Working in one every day then going home to isolation and misery every night was too much.

I kept my explanation brief for a couple of reasons. My need for self-preservation meant I was still reluctant to make noise and advocate for myself. I was scared to use my voice and share how his treatment made me feel. I didn't want to hear from yet another person that an experience that negatively impacted me didn't matter. I shared the bare minimum because I was emotionally vulnerable from every other part of my life and knew I couldn't handle my feelings being dismissed once again. Saying I couldn't handle the ongoing issues with my boss was all the truth I could muster.

I was fired the next day. It wasn't framed as a firing, of course. It was framed as them choosing to pay out my notice period without me coming to work. Fine by me.

Much like I had done just ninety days prior, I got on-line and applied to every single job I was qualified for in the Seattle area. Despite some early interest and a few phone screens, it was obvious I wasn't going to be starting a new job before my final check arrived from the old one. That's when the panic and then the deep depression started to set in.

I tried to listen to my friends and give myself some grace. It didn't work. I was much better at being the compassionate friend than I was at being kind to myself. In the span of just a few days, I had met DNA Dad, left my job, and was now facing financial ruin. I'd blown up my life for the second time in just over a year and my future was once again completely uncertain. What the hell was I doing? I had no idea.

I received an email from the CEO a few days after my firing. It was cc'd to their labor attorney, telling me they conducted a detailed, thorough investigation. It seems they talked to all parties and found no evidence to support my claims of mistreatment. Their detailed investigation did not involve a single interview with me, nor, as I later learned, any of the people who had reported similar issues. They'd circled the wagons and I had been dismissed. Literally and figuratively.

Meanwhile, Carl was continuing to push for more of a connection than I could handle. He wanted a best friend. He wanted a chance at the relationship he said was missing with his other daughters. And he wanted it at warp speed. It was too much. I was overwhelmed and struggled daily to cope with the pressure of being everything to a stranger I met once.

I mustered all the strength I had left to use my voice and ask him to pull back a little. He respected it and backed off for a handful of days before reverting to what felt like nonstop, pressured communication. Text messages would start as early as six in the morning and continue throughout the day. He called nearly every day, too. Sometimes I let it go to voicemail because I didn't have the energy to be there for him when I was barely able to be present for myself.

It was late summer. I was spending my days in an overstuffed chair in front of the TV, drinking ice water and eating chocolate ice cream. I spent my nights in front of the TV drinking vodka.

Summer turned to fall, and life kept getting worse. I was unemployed and broke, bordering on homeless. Interviews were going nowhere. I'd paid rent for three months straight by credit card. I paid everything else using cash advances from cards that were about to stop working. I was buried in debt from my business failing, and now my cards were nearly maxed. How rent was getting paid the next month was a mystery.

I forced myself to leave my apartment each day for lonely walks around the neighborhood or the lake. It was my only exercise aside from regular strolls downstairs to Total Wine. Sometimes it was the only contact I had with the outside world.

I put on a smile and positive attitude for my kids during our daily check-in calls but otherwise withdrew as much as I could. My days bled together in a daily routine defined only by which shows were on when. I started to wonder if trusting my intuition had been stupid and impulsive. Life had not improved since I started listening to it. But then, life also sucked when I didn't listen, so maybe my intuition was broken? Did it know anything at all? Or did it exist solely to keep me broke and alone?

Being connected to Carl grew more uncomfortable with each passing day. I had been assigned the role of marriage counselor on top of best friend and favorite secret daughter. He was losing patience with the fact that

I couldn't tell him I loved him or call him dad. I tried to explain that I didn't call anyone dad and that "I love you" to a father figure was hard for me. It fell on deaf ears. He wanted more than I could give, and what I needed stopped mattering days after our first conversation. The constant pressure to feel something I didn't and the expectation to give more than I had was unbearable. I started dreading the text alerts. Almost all the calls were sent straight to voicemail.

My friends and closest siblings continued to reach out. I engaged enough to make sure they knew I was still breathing then went right back to being a vodka-buzzed zombie in front of the TV.

During dinner with my brother Steven one night, I let my guard down and was candid about life. I shared that I'd been really depressed and one night, a couple of weeks earlier, had started writing goodbye notes to everyone. I was tired of being in pain, and I was tired of trying so hard to change my life but still feeling lonely and unhappy. I hated that at forty-nine, I was broke and living in a studio apartment I couldn't afford much longer. I had decades of experience in my field yet couldn't find a job in a market with the lowest unemployment rates in nearly fifty years. It was humiliating.

I felt so ashamed of where I was in life and how hard I was struggling. On the rare occasions I allowed myself to break down, I cried until the tears ran dry then I sat and stared off into nothing. I was scared it would never end. I was scared that I was destined to be alone and in pain no matter how hard I tried or how much work I did to heal. I genuinely believed it was always going to be this way, and I was so tired of fighting for a happy life that didn't seem to want me.

My logical brain knew from years of therapy that I deserved good things. I even knew the darkness I was feeling wouldn't last forever, but it didn't matter. My emotional brain was in charge and it wasn't sure I was destined for peace and happiness. After all, people don't always get the life they deserve, and maybe, for me, it just needed to be enough to know I deserved better. I needed to stop fighting and accept my reality. So, I gave up.

I surrendered to the nonstop pain and the darkest thoughts, and then I started making plans to say goodbye. I spent a few days convincing myself that if I explained it well enough to my kids, they would understand. That if I explained it to my friends and siblings that they, too, would understand. Truthfully, I didn't care what it would do to my mom. In my mind, at that time, it was fair repayment for a lifetime of lies.

In the end, as I explained to Steven over a shared dinner of roast chicken and mashed potatoes, it was the nights spent writing and rewriting the goodbyes that made me realize I didn't want to die. I just wanted the pain to stop. For me, that meant mentally shifting gears and accepting that despite all the work and all the trying, I just might not be destined for the type of love and happiness that seems to come so easily to others. I came to believe I was destined for contentment and a different kind of peace. I believed my future would likely be filled with meaningful relationships with my kids and my sacred circle of siblings and friends, but without a life partner. My next goal was to be okay with that.

My brother listened attentively as I bared my soul and explained it all. I was so grateful to have an evening out of the apartment talking with someone who knew me and would understand. I was past the heavy part, the scary part, and it felt like such a victory. I felt heard and seen for the first time in what felt like forever. My weeks of isolation and natural introversion, combined with the heavy emotional stuff I was in the middle of unpacking, meant the connection was more necessary than usual. We parted ways in the parking lot with a hug and "love you", which was not our norm. I drove home feeling warm and supported and cared for. Hopeful, even.

That night, I got a text from mom, the first communication of any kind in nearly three months. It said, "I love you." I smiled, thinking it meant she might finally be ready to have a real talk soon. I went to bed without responding.

My sister, Natasha, who lives nearby, reached out the next morning. She wanted to come visit and maybe take a wellness walk around the lake. It was early October. Watching the leaves change had ushered in a new season of my healing. I was still on an emotional support high from my brother and here was my sister, who rarely came to my place, offering to come to me instead of me driving to see her. I was surrounded in warmth from all the love.

She arrived with a bottle of water and tote bag with books and piles of paperwork overflowing. That seemed odd. Why bring homework to go for a walk? She was acting super weird, like something was on her mind, or had just happened, but she wasn't going to talk about it.

After a few minutes of unusually awkward chatting while she became more and more uncomfortable, she finally told me to sit down because she needed to tell me something. Turns out Steven had called Mom after our dinner to tell her I wasn't doing well, and he was worried. Mom called Natasha to say she was flying in today to check on me. Instead of a walk, my sister was here to offer support and to keep me from being blindsided by a drop-in from the single most emotionally unavailable person in my life. From the person who, whatever her intentions, had hurt me over and over again.

I felt so betrayed. I had opened myself up to my brother, who I felt safe with, who I thought understood, who

I thought heard what I was telling him, that I had gone through the darkness and I was coming out the other side, and he went straight to Mom. Mom, who has never once been comforting, who is the last person I needed or wanted to see at that moment. I struggled to hold in my emotions. My poor sister sat there staring in silence. She had never seen me broken and was unsure what to do other than be present. A lifetime of not being listened to and not having my feelings respected bubbled over. I was enraged that once again someone took my vulnerability and betrayed me. I was devastated that I couldn't even trust being open with my closest siblings without it somehow biting me in the ass.

I shook with rage. The betrayal and pain were ripping open my heart. "I had a couple of bad days a few weeks ago!" I cried. "I'm not suicidal! I'm fine! I don't want to see her! It won't help. Talking to her never does. I can't believe he'd do this. What the fuck was he thinking calling her?"

I just kept repeating myself while my sister looked at me helplessly. She had no idea what to do, but she wanted me to know she was here. My stomach ached like I'd been gut punched. My chest felt heavy and my head was reeling. I had worked very fucking hard my entire adult life to process the emotional shit storm that was my existence. Now the person responsible for creating most of it was on her way to regale me with martyred silence or, "I'm sorry, but I did what I had to do" repeated endlessly for the duration of her visit.

I was barely making it through one of the darkest times of my entire life. I didn't want to see my mom because I didn't want to feel the lifelong frustration of trying to be heard by a woman who is incapable of truly hearing me or acknowledging my pain. I didn't want to be dismissed or shut down again. She wasn't going to tell me the truth about anything, and she'd never accept responsibility for the lifetime of lies. What I needed from her was some accountability. An acknowledgment, at least, of the pain and confusion she'd caused. But that need didn't make sense to her, and she wouldn't, she couldn't, give it to me. Instead, this visit would be like walking into a room filled with knives and willingly backing into the sharpest one. Eventually all the wounds she had given me had reached my heart. I was raw, and I was hurt, and seeing her now would make it bleed all over again at a time when I was doing everything in my power to heal. To survive.

I didn't know what to do. I paced for a while then sat. Being still was impossible. So was moving around. I texted "we need to talk" to my brother. I tried to breathe and calm my racing heart. Eventually, shock took over and I went numb. I was mentally moving to survival and logistics mode, which meant rapid-fire questions.

> *She doesn't know where I live. Where did she get my address?*

> *How does she plan on getting in the building? It's secure, it's not like she can walk up to my front door and knock!*

> *What's she planning to do, ambush me in my own home? I don't get it! I don't understand why she's coming. Why couldn't she tell me she's coming over? Why does she do this? Why does she keep things from me? What if I wasn't home? What was her plan then?*

I had so many questions. Hundreds of them that all started with a single word: why.

My sweet sister didn't know how to provide support for a breakdown, but she kept sitting there in a silent show of love. Finally, I gave up and took a shower. By the time I was dressed and ready, I was calmer. Still enraged, but at least breathing normally again. Mom called Natasha a few minutes later to say she'd arrived then texted shortly after from the elevator. Some kind neighbor had let in the little old lady carrying the pink paisley backpack purse with the pocket hand sanitizer key ring and Mickey Mouse buttons pinned to the outside. To the outside world, she's harmless. To me, she's the wolf.

I opened the door at the first knock. It was the first time I'd seen her in six months. The expression on her face was a mix of fear, anticipation, and forlorn hero, here to save what no one else could. She gave me an awkward, empty hug then took a tour of my studio, deeming it "very nice" as though she were visiting a college student in their first apartment. My sister tried to make small talk while Mom made herself at home in my oversized chair. The lone piece of furniture in the place. I was at the kitchen counter, gripping it tightly to keep from going off on her. Mom retreats from confrontation, so any chance at answers this ambush visit held meant putting on kid gloves and treating her like the fragile flower she has never been.

I endured the casual conversation until I could handle it no more. "Why are you here, Mom?" I asked through gritted teeth. Staring at my knuckles as they whitened from their grip on the counter.

"If you don't want me here, I can leave", she replied in the same manipulative victim-like tone she always used when uncomfortable.

"I want to know why you're here. I haven't heard from you in months."

"You haven't called me, either", she said.

"You're right, I haven't. But you keep pumping the kids and everyone else for information on my life. If you want to know what's going on, ask me. Not them."

"Would you have talked to me if I tried?"

"Yes."

"I don't believe that. The last message you sent was that you weren't ready to have me back in your life yet. I still have it. Do you want me to show it to you?"

"No, Mom. I know what I said. What I want is to know why you're here."

"Your brother said you were having a hard time."

"I'm fine!" I practically yelled. All the fresh feelings of betrayal rushing back to the surface. "I had a bad couple of days, but I'm dealing with it and I am fine now. You didn't need to come over."

"That's good. I'm glad you're doing okay."

"I talked to Carl. You and his wife are a lot alike."

"I wouldn't know. I don't know him."

"That's a lie, Mom. You gave him my number."

"I called and gave him your number, but I haven't talked to him. I don't know anything about his life."

"Yeah well, I've talked to him, and you and his wife are a lot alike."

"Honey, you have to understand you're only getting his side of the story."

"That's because you won't tell me anything!" I was trying so hard to keep from screaming. "Tell me your side!"

"It doesn't matter. You're still going to believe what you want to believe."

And so, it went. Back and forth. Me asking, begging, pleading. Her adapting and deflecting without ever sharing a bit of information. This was her opportunity to comfort me. To ease my pain. She could have loved me enough to finally drop the lies and the clueless victim act. She could have chosen to tell the truth and have a real conversation. She didn't. She chose silence and martyrdom. Again.

My sister was doing her best to disappear into the background. It is only because of her that I didn't go off completely. I wanted to scream the things I've been carrying around all my life. I wanted to blast my mom with everything I knew and watch her be destroyed with her own lies. I wanted to break her down so she would finally give me what I wanted.

The logical part of my mind knew that would never happen. Nothing I said to her, no matter how loud or with how many tears shed, would make her be there for me the way I needed. I had to stop expecting the impossible.

"So, what do you want to do, Mom?"

"Are you guys hungry? We could get lunch."

That was it. The end of the real talk. I put my armor back on and we went out for Mexican where we talked about nothing of importance. I was fine with that. The sooner we could wrap up the ambush, the better.

After lunch, we said goodbyes in the parking garage of my building. She gave me one hundred dollars, another awkward hug, and whispered "sorry for all this" in my ear then got in the car and left before I could ask what, specifically, she was sorry for. The ambush, the lies, the inability to comfort, the refusal to help, or something else.

Stepping Away

The days after that were a blur. My depression was getting darker and deeper. I still forced myself to do the things required to keep myself from sliding into the black hole for good, but it was clear I needed time to get myself back together mentally. The walks and the journaling had become check-the-box activities. I did them because I knew I was supposed to. In the back of my mind, I hoped that if I kept doing all the things I was supposed to, someday life would start to turn around. I needed to believe that one day I'd wake up in less pain than the day before.

An anonymous delivery arrived from Amazon late one afternoon. Inside was a silver necklace with a pendant that said *faith*. I wore it almost daily, deciding it was a sign from the universe that the black hole I'd fallen into did indeed have a bottom.

I texted my brother John, who lives across the country and who understands me – and Mom – well. I told him all about the ambush, along with a quick rundown of everything that led to this point. He's very stoic by nature and not one to be overly emotional about much of anything. After I opened up and shared my story, his response was simple but loving. "Heartbreaking," he said. "I'm sorry."

Mom didn't reach out. I wanted to be surprised, but I wasn't. The part of me that still ached for a mommy was hurt, though. I kept flashing back to a conversation we'd had years earlier at a time when I was trying to get her to see how abandoned I'd felt my whole life. I told her I felt like I'd been sacrificed.

"Every time I try to get you to see how it was for me," I'd said, "you make excuses. It's always the same thing. You tell me you had other kids to look out for and you did what you had to do."

"That's true," she had replied, "You seemed like you didn't need anybody and were hard to deal with back then. You were always so angry."

"Did you ever ask yourself why?" My voice had raised, but I tried to stay calm so I could keep the conversation going. "You let the man you married treat me like crap. You turned a blind eye to how awful life was for me and made me out to be the bad kid."

"You weren't the bad kid."

"I know!" I'd exclaimed, frustrated that she still didn't understand.

"You're right," she'd finally admitted, looking defeated and ready to just get it out and be done. "I did sacrifice you. But not when you think. It was years earlier when I had to work nights and you spent so much time with babysitters. I felt bad, but you seemed okay, so I let it go."

That conversation was the closest she ever came to acknowledging what I'd been through and, more importantly, her role in it. In the end, we were only able to agree that she'd sacrificed her child's stability and security. That she had abandoned me every bit as much as the absent parent she liked to blame.

We'd always disagreed on the when and the why, and honestly, the reason didn't matter anymore because after a lifetime of lies, her disappearance after the ambush proved she was still willing to walk away when I needed her. That I still didn't matter.

Pictures

I'd never really had a dad before, so I wasn't sure what to expect when trying to connect to Carl. I certainly didn't know how to form a relationship with a man I'd just met, who was, whether he liked it or not, part of my messy, complicated history with my mom. From the start, I was uncomfortable with some of the things he said. I dismissed the red flags as my usual anxious, overthinking nature going into overdrive.

In our early phone calls, he would tell me every time how much I was wanted and loved. It felt inauthentic, though, like he was trying to fix a stranger's lifetime of daddy issues in a handful of phone calls. But then he would follow it up every single time by telling me he had no idea I existed until he got my letter. One of those things was obviously untrue.

The other problem was that he didn't know me, and not only because we had just met. He had a way of turning every conversation around, so we always ended up talking about him, or my mom. He wanted to talk to me all the time, but never wanted to talk *about* me. He wasn't curious about me or interested in my life. I honestly felt just as invisible talking with him as I'd felt most of my life. He didn't see me. He didn't hear me.

He also seemed weirdly fixated on my mom, even after all these years. He commented often on our resemblance and how he couldn't believe he had a daughter who was "so good lookin'." When he wasn't making comments about how similar we looked, he wasted my time saying a lot of nasty things about her, which made me angry. I am no fan of my mom's, but the man cheated on his wife every bit as much as she cheated on Gene. He was clearly no saint. Why should he get to dump it all on her like it wasn't something they did together? Honestly, it was all offensive. I was starting to feel like the fallout from a bad breakup. I'd spent a lifetime feeling unwanted, and I'd spent six years looking for this man. I didn't need to spend what little emotional bandwidth I had left listening to someone run his mouth about a relationship he had fifty years ago. He was also calling me behind his wife's back, which was a big red flag.

It became clear that he had issues with appropriate boundaries. He knew I was divorced and not dating anyone, and I'd mentioned more than once that I wasn't interested in it for the time being. He pressed the subject, telling me I should consider a casual, friends with benefits arrangement with someone. It was awkward and sort of gross. It wasn't the kind of conversation I wanted to have with anyone about my love life, but it was definitely not the dynamic of an adult child getting to know her father for the first time. I was always uncomfortable talking to him, no matter how hard I tried, no matter how often we talked. I felt constantly guarded and stressed. I hated it.

For my 49th birthday, Carl sent me an envelope of pictures of him throughout his life along with a letter. One of the pictures, a black and white shot of him at about five or six years old, stopped me cold. It was my face.

I'd spent my life resenting the constant comparisons to my mom. Even from Carl now, almost 50 years after the fact, it was the same thing: how much I looked like my mom. Over and over again people said it. But this picture left zero doubt that I am my father's daughter. I had two distinct reactions when looking at the pictures he sent and seeing, for the first time, an undeniable resemblance to someone other than my mother. My first thoughts were of my last visits with Gene as a young teenager, back when I still believed I was his. He never looked at me. At times, it felt like he actively went out of his way to avoid it. I had always assumed it was because I look like my mom, and maybe it was too painful. In looking at that picture, I wondered if that was the full truth. I wondered if what he really saw when he looked at me was Carl's face. Did Gene know, too? Did they both keep the truth from me? Did all three of them? I didn't know.

The other thing I realized was that I was done. I wasn't fed up or frustrated. Instead, what I knew was that I didn't need to pursue a relationship with Carl anymore. Seeing a lifetime's worth of pictures had somehow healed the wound. And, ultimately, it wasn't about finding a new father, it was about finding my identity. When I finally saw a face that looked like mine, when I finally knew the truth, that was enough.

After my Mom's disastrous ambush, Carl kept pushing me to come visit. The requests culminated with an invite to a fifty-first wedding anniversary party he and his wife were throwing for themselves. Their daughters were not attending. Nor were any of their extended family. He wanted me to go so he could introduce me as his daughter to all his friends. I didn't want to go. Being trotted out like a show pony would have been humiliating. I was horrified at the idea his wife would have to sit there while he showed off a secret daughter two years younger than his marriage vows. But it was important to him, so I defaulted to my old habits, ignored what I needed, and I told him I would try. I said this despite the fact that I hadn't felt so exhausted and emotionally defeated since my second divorce. All I really wanted to do was find a way to get through the day. I wanted nothing to do with anyone for any reason. That was especially true for strangers, regardless of shared DNA.

On top of all the personal life chaos, my job interviews weren't leading to offers and deep financial panic was closing in. Eviction, then homelessness, was less than thirty days away. The current crisis that was my life didn't seem to matter to Carl, so I tried again to rationalize away my feelings. "Carl is excited about having a new daughter," I told myself, "he wants to see me again. I just need to just suck it up and go. It'll make him happy." I told myself all these things but still didn't say yes to the invite. I was falling apart and didn't want to go. That's the truth that kept surfacing no matter how hard I tried to keep it down. The calls and messages did not let up. He didn't know about Mom's ambush and generally struggled to connect to my life, so it's not surprising that he didn't shift his focus. It was as frustrating and draining as ever, but not surprising.

I struggled hard with my feelings. I spent six years looking for a name and the truth. Now here it was – here *he* was – and everything about it made me uncomfortable. Eventually, I accepted my truth: we may share DNA, but we are not family. It was time to stop fighting for something that was not going to develop. It became obvious that the only way I could stay connected to Carl was if we had clear boundaries. So, I told him that I was overwhelmed and struggling. I said that I wanted to continue to talk to and get to know him, but I needed a break, so I was stepping away for a bit. I tried to reassure him that I was not disappearing and that I'd be back when I was in a better headspace. I said I needed to take care of myself and focus on getting better, which meant I would not be attending the anniversary party. I apologized and said I hoped he'd understand.

At first, he did. He thanked me for being honest, said he hoped I felt better soon and to reach out again when I was ready. It was such a relief, and I was proud of myself for speaking up. Unfortunately, his compassion proved short-lived. The next day, he said he changed his mind and did not understand anything. He let loose. Angrily accusing me of playing "fucking mind games," among other things. Through it all, he sounded less like a concerned parent and more like every other person in my life who expected me to ignore what I needed in favor of what they wanted.

After two more days of abuse, I blocked his number and felt relief for the first time since finding him.

Final Visit

The last time I saw Mom in person she was in the hospital for something avoidable and not life-threatening. It was November, a month after the ambush, and I was still figuring out my new boundaries with her. I decided to visit because it felt like the right thing to do. Practically speaking, I didn't want her to die without knowing I'd tried everything. I wasn't going to allow that to be another bit of guilt for me to bear for the rest of my life.

Mom was alone in her hospital room when I arrived. To anyone else, she'd look like someone's sweet grandmother, resting quietly under a pink fleece blanket with an IV line taped to the top of her right hand. To me, she looked like the living, breathing embodiment of lifelong deceit.

I felt no love when I looked at her, but no hate, either. I felt detached, as if looking at a stranger. I was still so angry inside but, finally, I had no interest in a fight. My need to battle her was done. I was at her bedside out of obligation and for my own peace of mind. I was not there for her.

"Hi Mom," I said when she saw me. "How are you feeling?"

"I'm better. I think they're sending me home today."

"Good," I replied, "I know how much you hate being in here."

She nodded. "Dad," she said, referring to my stepdad, "is out getting something to eat. He should be back in a little bit. How are you doing?"

"I'm fine."

"That's good. I'm glad to see you're doing better."

I sat across from the bed in the cheap vinyl chair provided for visitors, looking out the window at the city below. I wasn't sure what I wanted out of this visit and was starting to think I should leave.

"I am." I answered. "Work is good, and I'm not mad all the time anymore."

"I'm glad. You were always so angry," she said.

"Now we know why," I scoffed. "Being lied to my whole life will do that."

"I never lied to you, honey."

"You absolutely did."

"I did not!" She insisted. "You have to understand. I was young. I didn't know how biology worked."

I was incredulous. "Are you kidding me right now? You want me to believe you had no idea you could get pregnant by someone other than your husband? Is that the story you're sticking with?"

"It doesn't matter what I say. You'll never believe me."

She turned her head and refused to look at me. I watched her do what she always did when caught, withdraw deeper into her martyrdom. Convinced, as always, that the real victim is her.

"You're right," I said. "I'll never believe another word you say."

My stepdad came in a few moments later. Armed with a bagful of fast food and a super-sized iced tea, he had no idea about the conversation that had just transpired. The three of us chatted awkwardly until I decided I couldn't take it anymore.

"I need to get going," I said, raising up from the chair and gathering my things. "I'm glad you're feeling better." I hugged my stepdad and turned toward Mom.

"Thank you for coming by," she said. "It was good to see you."

I leaned down to give her a hug then kissed her cheek. I said, "I love you, Mom," and walked out the door.

~~~ Forgiveness, Peace, & Claiming my Soul

I started to feel a shift in the days before my fiftieth birthday. The constant heaviness of my soul was fading, and I was feeling lighter. Less weighed down by a lifetime of sadness, more filled with hope and a quiet joy.

It wasn't sudden. It's not like I woke up one morning to a magical epiphany and felt healed just because I was about to turn fifty. I'd learned long ago that healing doesn't work that way. Rather, it was a gradual sense of peace that slowly started to occupy more conscious space than the pain. I found I wasn't compelled to keep mining my past for fresh examples of trauma. I didn't need to find ways to revalidate my feelings. I was as the point where more digging was not going to lead to more understanding.

I knew I'd been physically, sexually, emotionally, and mentally abused. I knew I was raised by, and then married to, a narcissist. I knew I'd loved people who were wrong for me and who could never love me back. And, most importantly, I knew I'd survived it all.

A lifetime of trauma had affected every piece of who I am – and how I am – in the world. That truth was indisputable. Because of that, I no longer needed to explain or justify or debate people who may or may not have the ability to understand. My trauma and recovery were as real and true as the freckles on my face or the scars on my body. I didn't need to wear it on my sleeve for the world to see as proof to make it so.

Instead of wearing my trauma, I now have a white ink tattoo on my forearm with the words *I forgive myself* written in Sanskrit. I chose white ink because it's for me, not the world, and Sanskrit because it's beautiful and peaceful. It is my reminder to give myself the grace and love I'd spent my life searching for in others.

I took ownership of my story. It's mine and mine alone to share. One of the keys to my freedom was realizing not everyone was worthy. If I choose to share, it's because I want someone to see and know me a little more deeply. I don't need someone to validate me anymore because I've done the work to validate myself. Simply put, the truth and the past no longer hurt.

As I continued to rebuild my life, I started to unfollow some of the social media pages dedicated to childhood trauma, narcissistic abuse, and understanding addiction. Not all of them, because I still find comfort and strength in knowing the community is there, but it no longer needed to be front and center in my daily feed.

Around the same time, I noticed the simmering rage and resentment I felt toward my mom was gone. For the first time in as long as I can remember, I wasn't mad at her. She did what she did for reasons only she knows. That's her stuff to make peace with, not mine. I know now that she loves me. I also know she is incapable of honest, reflective accountability. Both of those things are true and because of that, she's forfeited the right to be part of my life going forward. I knew I was healed when I realized that decision wasn't punitive. It was protective. A boundary. What I needed outweighed whatever sense of entitlement she felt toward me and my world.

I love my mom. I want her safe, happy, and healthy. I want her to find peace. I also know I have zero control over any of those things, so I send my wants out to the universe and let it go.

The same philosophy goes for Carl. I'm sure he's a kind and lovely man who saw his life upended by a secret daughter he may or may not have known about. But his past relationship with my mom and the current state of his marriage are not my business. Neither is his bond with his other daughters. My need to dig ended when I found him, so I let go.

During my decades-long journey, I discovered that part of learning who I am meant a need to change my name, and to make the outside match the evolution happening inside. Truthfully, I had no deep emotional attachment to the names I'd used throughout my life. They were given by men who were not there for me the way I needed. But I'd done the work. I kept showing up for myself, and honoring that was important. Given how hard that battle was, it would have been a betrayal to continue using someone else's. Choosing my own was a way of saying, "See me, I am here." I remember having tears in my eyes the day I explained to a judge that I was changing my name because I no longer wanted my ex-husband's. My identity is my own now. I am beholden to no one.

I learned that I am more than my trauma and my past. More than the best things I have done, the choices I have made – good and bad – or the worst things done to me. I know now that bad things happen to good people, and sometimes good people do bad things. True, lasting peace and forgiveness has meant accepting it all.

For the last two years, I have relied on my friends more than at any other time in my life. They have shepherded me through storm after storm with unending love and support. One reminds me regularly to give myself grace and breathe. While I'm sure they have all wished that over the years, she is the one who spells it out straight. This sacred circle of friends is who I turn to when the noise gets loud and I need a reminder that this, too, shall pass.

I used to believe I was broken. I just knew something in me was defective because growing up I'd had such a hard time connecting and forming emotional bonds. Walking away from people was the easiest thing in the world. It barely took any thought at all. What I know now is that it was self-preservation and a learned trauma response to my environment. It was not a failure or a character defect. It was survival. And it was not uncommon.

It wasn't until I became a mother that I realized I could easily hand my heart over to another person. Raising my boys, and being a good parent, became the first thing I believed without question I could do well. I needed no external validation. Truthfully, I didn't give a shit what anyone thought about me as a mom. I trusted myself and my bond with my kids and chose to tune out all the noise. It worked.

Over the years, while I was raising them, that confidence in my own judgement started to carry over to my friendships. I stopped questioning why people wanted to spend time with me and started trusting how I felt when deciding if I wanted to spend time with them. I gained and lost friends over the years, but the ones who truly saw me are the ones who stayed.

What I have now is a family I have created for myself. I share DNA with some, not with others. I have never believed that DNA is what creates a family, so this circle of chosen family is built on the foundations that truly matter. I am surrounded by people who love me unconditionally, and I them. Through them, I have learned I am capable of genuine, intimate connections with people. I can open my soul, lie bare my deepest vulnerabilities, and trust every single one of them to honor it and handle with care. It is the gift of a lifetime, and one I can never repay.

In the end, I learned the details and specifics of my trauma and abuse were unique but not special. Something about discovering that so many others had survived and thrived after working through their own histories gave me courage. Taking the time to learn about the psychology of abuse, narcissism, and addiction armed me with knowledge. Using the tools gained from years of hard work with talented therapists got me through the hard days. Meditation, yoga, and long solo walks quieted the noise. Leaning on my circle surrounded me with love. Feeling it all with no expectation or judgement let me move through the darkness and into the peace. Forgiving and trusting myself allowed me to finally be free.

I had claimed my soul.

Acknowledgements

Unclaimed Soul began as a journal. It was my way of trying to make sense of the waves of conflicting emotions that left me exhausted and feeling like I was drowning. As I wrote, I began to notice that deep pain and insecurity were the common threads interwoven throughout my history. It also became clear that I needed to view my life and experiences holistically rather than as a series of isolated, unrelated events.

Since the parent-child bond is the beginning of everything, I had to start with my mom. My story does not need a villain, though, and this book is not an indictment of her. My intention was simply to tell my truth and shine a light on what happens when secrets and fear collide with unresolved trauma. Intergenerational pain is impactful and complex. It can, and does, coexist with very real - and very true - love.

Thank you to Kristie Gow, Quinndara Woodworth, and Randy Garrett, the amazing therapists I have worked with over the years. I am deeply grateful. Without the dedicated and focused work done with each of you, I would not have found my way.

I am profoundly blessed to be surrounded by a group of friends and family too numerous to name. You know who you are, and I love you all. Thank you for loving and accepting me exactly as I am.

To my favorite humans, you are perfect, and I love you. Thank you for choosing me to be your mom and for understanding that I always get the last Dr Pepper.

Kari Grambo, my genius editor, thank you for the weekly chats and for pushing me to be ever more real and vulnerable. You are the reason this reads like a story and not a bunch of disjointed journal entries.

And finally, thank you to Krish Singh, Auctus Publishers, and Nikki MacCallum, for being cheerleaders and believing in the book in its earliest forms.

CPSIA information can be obtained
at www.ICGtesting.com
Printed in the USA
FSHW021555070821
83748FS

9 781736 827802